# Honey, I'm Home for Good!

**The ABCs of lovin' and livin' with your stay-at-home hubby**

# FOCUS ON THE FAMILY®

**Honey, I'm Home for Good!**

**The ABCs of lovin' and livin' with your stay-at-home hubby**

## Mary Ann Cook

### TYNDALE

Tyndale House Publishers, Inc.
Wheaton, Illinois

HONEY, I'M HOME FOR GOOD!

A Focus on the Family book published by Tyndale House Publishers, Wheaton, Illinois.

Editor: John Duckworth
Cover design: Peak Creative
Cover illustration: Dennis Jones

**Library of Congress Cataloging-in-Publication Data**
Cook, Mary Ann, 1943-
    Honey, I'm home for good! / Mary Ann Cook.
        p. cm.
Includes bibliographical references
      ISBN 1-58997-108-6
  1. Wives—Religious life. 2. Christian women—Religious life.
3. Wives—Effect of husband's retirement on. 4. Wives—Effect of husband's employment on. 5. Home labor. I. Title.
BV4528.15 .C66 2003
248.8'435—dc21

                                    2002156608

Printed in the United States of America

03 04 05 06 07 08 09/10 9 8 7 6 5 4 3 2 1

*This book is dedicated to my mother, who was so convinced that someday I would become a published author that she saved a copy of my third grade attempt, Mystery at Dungeon Hill—a blatant knockoff of the Bobbsey Twins series.*

◎◎

*I shall forever be grateful to you for having taught me by example that you can always find something to laugh about, even in the midst of difficulties.*

# Contents

# Acknowledgments

To my husband, Ken, whose decision to work from home is the inspiration behind this book: Thanks for letting me share our story in order to encourage others.

To my computer guy, my son Derrick, who never once rolled his eyes or muttered, "Mom, is it really that hard to understand?": Thanks for your help and your enthusiasm. Thanks also to Marsha and Aaron for lending your husband and daddy to me.

To my daughter, Kelly, thanks for your encouragement and for teaching me to write tighter sentences. (Make that, "for *trying* to teach me.")

A big "Thank you" to my friend and fellow writer, Debby Rau, whose keen editing skills shaped my rough draft into a marketable manuscript. I owe you big time!

I am also indebted to the men and women who shared their spouse-in-the-house stories with me, either at my seminars or in the supermarket aisles. Thanks for allowing me to use them in this book.

A huge "Thank you" to my cheerleaders: the dear ladies in Serendipity Bible Study; the San Diego Christian Writers' Guild, especially the Escondido Critique Group; my ministry team at Sunbridge West Care Center; my pastor, Bruce Humphrey; and last, but absolutely not least, all of my faithful girlfriends. What a blessing you all are to me!

Finally, to my editor, John Duckworth, and all the caring folks at Focus on the Family. Thanks for your patience with this first-time author. I appreciate your gentle guidance.

# Introduction

⟨⊘⟩

*Marriages are made in heaven;*
*so are thunder and lightning.*
—Author unknown

# 1

# Ready or Not

⨪⨪

*If you don't learn to laugh at trouble,*
*you won't have anything to laugh at when you're old.*
—EDGAR HOWE

On a sunny September afternoon in 1992, I was preparing to place a meatloaf in the oven when my husband bounded through our kitchen door with a large box in his hands.

"Hi, Honey—I'm home!" he shouted as he set the mysterious box on our kitchen table. Then, with all the flair of a magician pulling a rabbit out of a hat, he reached into the deep confines of the box and excavated a fax machine.

"And thanks to this baby, I'm home for good," he announced with a grin. He set the technological wonder on the table and gave it a little pat. "I'll be able to telecommute from home and avoid that awful freeway commute. I may even have time to do some consulting work on the side."

This surprise announcement of his intent to work from home caused me to drop the platter I was holding. As I stared at the broken chunks of china and mounds of ground beef splattered across the floor, I thought, *My life—like that platter —will never be the same again.*

And it hasn't.

Gradually, though, I've been able to fit most of the pieces (of my life, not the platter) back together again. A few chips and cracks remain, but I'm still functional. The glue that holds me together is my faith and a sense of humor. On particularly trying days when I'm close to tears and find myself muttering, "Lord, give me strength," He does. Then He goes one step further and points out the humor in my situation— so that I end up laughing instead of crying.

If your spouse is retired or working from home, and it's creating friction, you may not see anything humorous about your life. Whether you're a homemaker, retiree, or career woman with an office under your own roof, if your husband is suddenly underfoot, you're probably struggling with the adjustment. Irritations like too much togetherness or a lack of privacy may make it hard for you to see anything funny about your situation.

But I promise that someday you'll be able to find some humor in having an at-home husband—maybe even before you've finished reading this book! To help you make that adjustment, I've developed a system I call the ABCs of Coping. The letters stand for . . .

- Accepting Your Situation
- Bettering Your Situation
- Cherishing Your Situation.

## Cherish Is the Word?

Right now you may be yelling, "*Cherish* my situation? Are you nuts? Do you have any idea what I'm going through?"

Believe me, I do. As a work-from-home writer and speaker, I face many of the same challenges. Here's an example.

For the last 30 minutes I've been seated at the computer in my office, with the door closed. During this time, my husband has knocked twice—once to inform me that the weatherman is predicting rain on Saturday, then again to ask if I have anything that needs to be mailed. This happens every weekday at 10:25 A.M. Thanks to my spouse's predictability, I never need to phone the "time lady." Before making his usual trek to the post office at precisely 10:30, he checks the outgoing mail basket on our kitchen desk at precisely 10:25 and inquires, "Do you have anything to mail?"

"If I do, it's in the basket," I answer, right on cue.

"Just checking to be sure," he replies.

Do I cherish these interruptions? Of course not. Am I grateful to have my own personal meteorologist and courier? You bet.

Perhaps the word *cherish* is too strong. Try thinking of it as "being grateful" for your situation. (See, I have this little alliteration thing going with the ABCs of Coping and I need a "C" word instead of a "G" word.)

## From Complaining to Compassion

I confess that being grateful was not an immediate reaction to my new situation. In the early stages of my husband's eternal presence, I spent hours complaining about my plight to anyone who would listen—the lady standing behind me in the grocery line, fellow shoppers at the mall, my dog's vet—anyone with ears. I discovered that just about everybody had a spouse-in-the-house story to tell.

After a while I decided that instead of holding support group sessions in grocery stores where they impeded traffic flow, we fellow strugglers needed to find a less crowded spot to share our house-spouse stories. So I called the local community college to pitch the idea of teaching a class on the subject of adjusting to a spouse's retirement or work-at-home status. It was an easy sale, since the director's father had recently retired. "He's driving my mom crazy," she confided.

Now that I had a meeting room, I faced the question of what to say to the group. Surely I had plenty of stories to fill the three-hour class—but since the women would be paying a small fee to attend, they deserved more than a three-hour gripe session. After all, they had plenty of friends and family members whose ears they could bend for free. What they needed were some skills to help them deal with their husbands' daily presence—or on preparing for the inevitable event if it hadn't come yet.

So I did further research, talking not only to fellow wives, but to professional counselors and pastors. The result was the ABCs of Coping.

Here's how the ABCs work. Once you make it through the toughest part, "Accepting," you move on to "Bettering"— where all the practical stuff is. And though you may not believe it now, you'll eventually reach the point where you can "Cherish" (or at least be grateful for) your situation—even if it's only for the fact that you now have someone around to carry in the groceries.

You'll also begin to develop compassion for your spouse as you start to consider *his* side of the story. This is especially important for those with retired husbands. Psychologists say that, for men, the stress of retirement ranks right up there with life's three major stressors—puberty, death, and divorce. The retired husband often struggles with the fact that he's no longer welcome in his workplace. He also must figure out where and how he fits in at home. He may feel like the new kid on the block, sensing that you perceive him as moving in on your territory. Resolving these conflicts may depend on whether you can drag that welcome mat from its hiding place in your closet and let your husband know that you love and value him not for what he does (or no longer does), but for who he is.

In my workshops I ask the ladies to keep a "gratitude journal." They begin by writing down five things about their spouses for which they're grateful. Everyone finds this an easy assignment. I know you will, too.

It's been said that there are two ways of meeting difficulties: You alter the difficulties or you alter yourself to meet them. You'll need to do a little of both as you adjust to your husband's being at home for good.

Why not give the ABCs of Coping a shot?

Let's start with . . . Accepting.

# PART I

# Accepting Your Situation

෧෧

*Life is not a problem to be solved,*
*but a gift to be enjoyed.*
—JOSEPH P. DOOLEY

# 2

# Here to Stay

@/@

*My wife and I had words—*
*but I didn't get to use any of mine.*
—FIBBER McGEE

Since it was a Friday when my husband, Ken, announced his
intentions of working from home, I didn't immediately notice
the effects of his decision. After all, I was used to having him
around the house on weekends.

But Monday told a different story. After I saw my two
children off at the front door, I turned to find my husband still
standing beside me. Dressed in sweats and clutching a coffee
cup, he smiled as he watched our children depart. It took a
moment for my brain to process the scene: no suit, no tie, no
briefcase. *He's not going anywhere!* I thought.

Not quite knowing what to do with this information, I
decided to continue my usual morning routine. I poured
myself a cup of tea and grabbed the crossword puzzle from
the newspaper. Seated on the living room couch, engrossed in

the clues for "1 across," I heard Ken exclaim, "Aha! So *this* is what you do all day!"

Well, them thar were fighting words—so I launched a few missiles in retaliation. "For your information," I shouted, "I have been up since dawn, fed the kids, fixed their sack lunches, and put a load of laundry in. So if it's all right with Your Majesty, I will take a few moments to myself!"

"Whoa, lighten up!" Ken pleaded, backing away. "I was only kidding." Then he made a mad dash for the safety of his den.

He was right, of course. I did need to lighten up. But it wasn't going to be easy. I was used to my privacy and my laid-back lifestyle. My husband, on the other hand, was used to being organized and having every day planned.

I began to feel as if I were in prison, my every move under the scrutiny of the warden. If Ken caught me watching Oprah in the middle of the afternoon, I felt as guilty as if he had discovered a hidden weapon in my cell.

In order to look busy, I started carrying a broom with me at all times. I got this idea from comedienne Phyllis Diller, who had described a slightly different ploy for excusing her home-making habits. She kept a supply of "get well" cards in a drawer in case company arrived unexpectedly. Then she would grab the cards and display them on her mantel so that she could lament, "Excuse my messy house, but I have been ill."

Of course, this charade with the broom did not fool Ken. He began to help out around the house. I should have been grateful for his help, but took it as an affront to my house-keeping skills.

"I was just going to do that," I would say defensively when he filled the ice trays or emptied the wastebaskets.

This went on for months, until a friend intervened. Tired of hearing me complain about how Ken had taken over my household, she said, "So what? Are you really so fond of housework that you can't bear to give some of it up?"

"Well, duh, no!" as my teenage daughter would say. In fact, I agree with Erma Bombeck's view of housework: "My second favorite household chore is ironing. My first being hitting my head on the top bunk until I faint."

I realized my husband was home to stay. I could either waste my energy railing against that fact, or I could accept it and find a way to make it work for good. One way of "working it for good" would be to let Ken take over a few of my chores. I did have better things to do with my time.

## I'm Not the Only One

One of the first things I did with my free time was to write an article for *Today's Christian Woman* magazine, entitled "Make Room for Dad." The humor piece chronicled the difficulties our entire family encountered while trying to adjust to my husband's decision to work from home. Our children, both teenagers at the time, were feeling the repercussions of Ken's daily presence as much as I was. It was fine to have Dad monitor their actions on the weekend, but it was a real drag to have a full-time father around, especially when he objected to their loud music and frequent phone calls. To make matters worse, my husband—bless his heart—was eager to make up for all those years of commuting when he'd had neither the time nor energy to spend with his kids. He didn't realize that his "kids" were 13 and 18 and not exactly thrilled to hang out with Dad—or Mom, for that matter.

When the article on our struggles was published, I was amazed at the requests for reprints—which came from as far away as Germany. I'd had no idea that conflicts in families with at-home husbands were so widespread.

## Are We Just Wimps?

Is Spouse-in-the-House Syndrome just another invention of the current Whiny Generation? After all, if having an at-home husband is such a problem, why haven't we heard a word about it from our parents or grandparents?

The answer is simple: longevity and technology. Thanks to modern medicine, people are living 10 to 12 years longer than they used to. In the old days, when a couple promised "till death do us part," death came pretty quickly. As anthropologist Margaret Mead put it, "That is why it seemed that marriages lasted forever. In the old days everyone was dead."[1]

Now marriages spill over into the retirement years, that period once described as "twice as much husband and half as much income." It's predicted that many baby boomers will live for another two decades after reaching the age of 65. Then there's the growing trend of early retirements. According to U.S. government statistics, the average age at which retired men went on Social Security in 1997 was 63.7, down from 68.7 in 1950; for women, the ages were 65.4 and 68, respectively.

As for technology, the ability to work from home via computer and fax machine has given a whole new meaning to the term "home office." Score another one for science!

So now women are saying, "Hey, I married you for better or worse, but not for lunch every day."

Now you know why you're in your present situation, faced with the possibility of fixing your husband a daily sandwich—and maybe longing for the life you used to know.

## Good Grief

In some ways, adjusting to an at-home husband mirrors the grief process. I grieved for the loss of my old lifestyle. For a long time I was stuck in the first phase of grieving, denial. I hoped against hope that I'd wake up and find that my life had returned to the way it had been when my husband was gone from 6 A.M. to 6 P.M. I even visualized the good fairy waving her wand to make my husband disappear.

As long as I remained stuck in denial, I would never be able to get on with my life. I needed to follow two popular teenage adages: "Get over it!" and "Get a life!"

## Four Keys to Acceptance

How could I accept what was happening so that I could move ahead with my life? In time I recognized four important facts that helped me get started on the path to acceptance:

1. The man I viewed as a home invader was simply the husband I'd promised to love and cherish "till death do us part."

2. "My house" was actually "our house." Mortgage papers don't lie.

3. I wasn't alone in my struggles. Women worldwide were going through the same kind of transition.

4. This new stage in my life was just that. It was not a form of punishment, but a natural occurrence.

As Barbara Silverstone and Helen Kandal Hyman explain in their book *Growing Older Together*, "Like the tide, a marriage or partnership is ever changing. It will go through a series of transitions, constantly readjusting and readapting according to the demands of each new stage in life. Most partnerships have ups and downs, alternating highs and lows. . . . Few relationships can sustain uninterrupted bliss. . . ."[2]

Anne Morrow Lindbergh echoed this idea in *Gift from the Sea*:

When you love someone you do not love them all
the time, in exactly the same way, from moment to
moment. It is an impossibility. It is even a lie to pre-
tend to. And yet this is exactly what most of us
demand. We have so little faith in the ebb and flow
of life, of love, of relationships. We leap at the flow
of the tide and resist in terror its ebb. . . . Security in
a relationship lies neither in looking back to what it
was in nostalgia, nor forward to what it might be in
dread or anticipation, but living in the present relationship and accepting it as it is now.[3]

## The Road to Contentment

So are you ready to accept your life as it is right now? Are you
ready to get over it?

Perhaps it's not enough to realize that this stage is a natural part of life for which medicine and technology share part
of the credit, or blame. Maybe it's not enough to know that
others are going through the same struggles. But it may help
to remember that God knows about, cares about, and can do
something about your turmoil.

The apostle Paul, who had plenty to complain about,
wrote, "I have learned to be content whatever the circumstances. . . . I have learned the secret of being content in any
and every situation. . . . I can do everything through him who
gives me strength" (Philippians 4:11-13).

Ask for His help. And keep reading.

# 3

# Howdy, Pardner

⊚⁄⊚

*This is a perfect pair—he's a
hypochondriac and she's a pill.*
—AUTHOR UNKNOWN

Jeff has been in the "work world" for decades. His wife,
Tamara, has been at home during this time. Jeff is used to giving orders at the office; Tamara has become the CEO of the
household. The house runs according to her schedule; she
decides what meals to serve, how the shelves and closets
should be organized, and what purchases to make.

This arrangement has worked well for years. But then
Jeff—due to retirement or telecommuting—returns home. It's
tough for him to relinquish his role as supervisor. He starts to
question Tamara's actions. He has a better idea for just about
everything, including the organization of her kitchen cabinets.
One day, the happy housewife reaches for the jar of oregano on
the shelf above the stove and finds a year's supply of paper
towels instead. The happy housewife is happy no more.

Does this scenario sound familiar? Then you and your mate should start thinking about ways to share the decision-making process. It's time to sit down and discuss the idea of forming a partnership.

## The Dreaded "C" Word: Compromise

Marital partnerships don't seem to come naturally. We balk at give-and-take because we assume we'll be doing all the giving while our mate does the taking. That's the conclusion of pastor Terrence Sherry of Fullerton, California, who told me, "We all know that in marriage we become one, but *which* one? Our fear . . . is that we will become the other one; that somehow we will become diminished. We don't realize that we can still maintain our separate identities, we are still two people in one marriage."

Or as writer Susan Littwin puts it, we are "individuals together, two distinct peas, now in a slightly different pod."[1] It's bound to get pretty uncomfortable in that little pod if we don't learn to compromise.

It helps if you have a sense of humor. My sister recently steered her overly helpful husband out of the kitchen and into their garage, where she presented him with a supply of organizational tools. His favorite was the labeling gun, and he went crazy with it. He labeled the contents of every drawer and shelf in the garage. On the pegboard over his workbench he carefully spelled out the name of the tool designated for each hook. He was in organizational heaven—until my sister sneaked into the garage one night and confiscated his labeling gun. She carefully clicked out the letters C-A-R and stuck this label on the hood of his BMW. His bicycle was next. My brother-in-law got the point and hung up his gun for good—on the hook marked "labeling gun," of course.

A friend tells me that when it comes to compromising with her husband, she finds it best to give in quickly on small issues but remain firm on the big ones that really matter to her. "Because I'm usually so agreeable," she explains, "when my husband sees a spark of stubbornness in me, he realizes that this is something I care a lot about and he is more willing to let me have my way."

## To Each His Own

Sometimes partnership means relinquishing a task that's always been yours, especially if your spouse is better suited for it.

Make an appointment with your husband to sit down and identify your respective areas of expertise. If you're the one doing all the cooking, for example, it probably makes sense for you to decide on how the kitchen will be organized. On the other hand, if your husband shows culinary talent, be sure to take into consideration his needs and desires.

Dr. Norm Wakefield, in his book *Men Are from Israel, Women Are from Moab*, illustrates the value of specializing in strengths:

> God has blessed each person with a toolbox of specially designed tools called gifts, talents, and abilities. Each person's toolbox looks a little different from the next. You may have tools such as hospitality, encouraging words or even humor. Another may have a toolbox filled with financial understanding, a keen business sense or an eye for details. When facing a dilemma, the submissive heart will allow the person with the right tools to fix the problem![2]

Dr. Wakefield suggests thinking of submission as a "Yield" sign in a relationship. Just as there are times when we need to yield to other drivers on the road, there are times when yielding to another's expertise is wise. He concludes, "Submission is give and take."[3]

After 52 years of marriage, Dr. Don Buteyn and his wife, Marian, are experts at majoring in their strengths. When they took a trip to Europe, Marian suggested, "Honey, you take care of the scheduling and let me decide what we are going to see."

"This was fine with me," Don says. "She would tell me where we needed to be, and I would figure out how to get there." He believes this was a good decision because "men seem more aware of the clock and feel a need to decide what needs to take place to get us from point A to point B."

## Who's the Boss?

But what happens when you and your spouse don't agree on who should do what? In *Getting to Yes: Negotiating Agreement Without Giving In*, authors Roger Fisher and William Ury suggest you focus on interests rather than positions. "Your position is something you've decided upon. Your interests are what caused you to so decide. Interests are what motivate people; they are the silent movers behind the hubbub of positions."[4]

If, for example, your husband insists on making the final decision on all major household purchases, ask yourself why. Put yourself in his shoes. What is it he enjoys about making such decisions? Does he like the research involved, or is he interested in the mechanics of the refrigerator or dishwasher?

Perhaps he thinks his knowledge of the inner workings of the products makes him the wiser one when it comes to purchases. If so, tactfully remind him that if you're the one using the refrigerator, you're the logical one to make the decision—even if you don't know what makes it tick! You know how many shelves you need, which models are easiest to clean, and whether a top freezer would be more convenient than a lower one. These are your interests, behind your position, which he needs to understand.

If your spouse still refuses to give in, don't make matters worse by being bullheaded. As Joyce Meyer points out in *Help Me, I'm Married!*, "When you demand your own way, you are the one who ends up suffering more than anybody else." She suggests that you "determine in your heart that you will take a new look at every disagreement you have with your spouse to see what God can do for you if you come together in agreement."[5]

She adds, "You can have such fun in your marriage when you begin to agree with each other."

If your spouse balks at the idea of a partnership because he still wants to be the El Supremo that he once was at the factory or office, remind him of successful corporate partnerships like Hewlett-Packard, Barnes & Noble, and Ben & Jerry's (*don't* mention Montgomery Wards). It wouldn't hurt to get out the dictionary and read him this definition of partnership: "A relationship . . . involving close cooperation between parties having specified and joint rights and responsibilities."[6] That sounds a lot like a marital relationship, doesn't it? After all, another term for spouse is marriage *partner*.

In time, your mate probably will come to see that a partnership is the only way to go. This is especially true in retirement. As psychiatrist Mark Goulston explains, "The jobs are gone, the children aren't around anymore. Couples know that if they are to age gracefully, they have to stick together. Necessity is the mother of cooperation."[7]

## Disagreeing Agreeably

In spite of your best efforts to cooperate and compromise, however, there will still be times in your marriage—as in any partnership—when you and your spouse can't agree. Disagreement is not always a bad thing, so don't despair.

That's the perspective of Ruth Bell Graham, who wrote, "Everyone needs to be disagreed with occasionally. There is danger when someone gets into a position of political or social power and no one dares to disagree. . . . We can disagree without being disagreeable."[8]

Be gracious when butting heads with your spouse, and remember that old proverb: "One side always sounds right, until you hear the other side."

Before beginning partnership negotiations with your husband, try reviewing the fruit of the Spirit—love, joy, peace, patience, kindness, goodness, faithfulness, gentleness, and self-control (Galatians 5:22-23). These attributes are worth striving for. A few verses further, you'll find a great motto for a successful marriage partnership: "Since we live by the Spirit, let us keep in step with the Spirit" (v. 25).

## When Your Marriage Needs Work

Of course, the future success of your marriage partnership depends a lot on the condition of your marriage before your husband started spending so much time at home. If you had a "good" marriage only because your husband was away most of the time, the two of you naturally will have a harder adjustment than a highly compatible couple who longed to spend more time together.

Do you need to spend some time building up a marriage that deteriorated while your husband was caught up in work and you immersed yourself in your children, household, or career? Try discovering each other through the dating process again. Ask each other questions as you did when you first met, so that you can determine each other's current interests.

Make a conscious effort to be the thoughtful, caring person you were in the early days of your relationship. Compile a list of things to do on a date, including activities that were fun for the two of you in the past.

I know one man who goes all-out on "date night" with his wife. He actually gets in his car, drives around the block, parks at the curb in front of their house, and goes to the door to pick up his wife. This romantic husband was just starting to plan for retirement when I first met him several years ago; I wasn't surprised to learn in a recent phone call that he and his wife are thoroughly enjoying their at-home years. "We are still joined at the hip," he told me.

Perhaps you don't feel quite as cheerful about the idea of being joined at the hip. Maybe you're suffering from over-familiarity. You know what they say about couples becoming as comfortable with each other as an old pair of shoes. But how appealing is that? Slip off those old shoes and kick up your heels!

Find a way to put some fun back into your relationship. Here are some ideas:

- If your husband is home on weekdays, take advantage of it. Theaters and restaurants are less crowded at that time, and many offer discounts. Enjoy a matinee and lunch, or an "early bird" dinner. Or pack a picnic lunch and head for the hills, park, lake, or beach.
- If you and your spouse are collectors, browse antique shops or visit garage sales. Treasure hunts are more fun if you have a specific item in mind, so make a wish list.
- Become tourists in your hometown, visiting local historic sites, museums, and scenic spots.
- Live near an amusement park? If your health permits, get in line for roller coasters, corn dogs, and cotton candy.

- Try to do at least one new thing together each week—even if it's as simple as attending the opening of a supermarket. When a new one opened near us, Ken and I spent a morning munching on free samples and familiarizing ourselves with the aisles. With his background in grocery stores, Ken especially enjoyed this outing—and saw our visit as research for future trips.

If you and your spouse have grown apart, jump-start your communication. In her book *Keys to Living with a Retired Husband*, Gloria Bledsoe Goodman offers the following conversation starters:

*If we could do anything we want today, what would it be?*

*If we could do anything we want for a week, what would you want it to be?*

*If we could do anything we want for the rest of our lives, what do you think it should be?*[9]

Notice that none of these questions can be answered with a simple yes or no. They require serious thought about goals and desires—as well as openness and honesty. Your answers may not match, but you'll begin to explore each other's likes and dislikes. You'll be on your way to forging a more compatible relationship.

## Beware of Power Plays

Once your relationship is on track, you can develop a healthy partnership. Even the best partnerships, however, can be derailed by hazards. One of them is the power play.

One common power play involves the car. The husband, for example, might arrange a lube job on the day that his wife planned a shopping spree with her friends. Did he do this because he truly forgot about her plans? Or is he lonely and wants his wife to stay home with him?

Or does he believe a woman's place is in the home, and he's determined to keep her there? As a Christian, I believe the husband is the spiritual head of the household, and I'm aware that many of us promised in our wedding vows to "obey." But our husbands also promised to cherish us. I know of some retired men who insist on chauffeuring their wives everywhere and won't allow them to drive at all.

This power play thing works both ways, of course. Wives can dabble in bossiness as much as husbands do. You don't want your spouse to be like the man who placed this ad in the *New York Times*:

> FOR SALE BY OWNER: Complete set of Encyclopedia Britannica. 45 volumes. Excellent condition. $1,000.00 or best offer. No longer needed. Got married last weekend. Wife knows everything.

According to one man, power-playing wives drive some men to take up model railroading. "It's not because they have regressed to their childhood," he explained, "but because it's the only thing they can control."

## Help—You Need Somebody

If, in spite of your best efforts to form a partnership, you and your husband find yourself arguing over everything and unable to reach any compromises, seek professional help from your pastor or a marriage counselor. There is no shame in admitting you need assistance in adjusting to this new stage in your lives. Sadly, one pastoral counselor told me that although he is aware of several couples in his congregation who are struggling with these issues, they have not sought his advice. He believes this is because the older generation is not as candid about its problems as younger couples tend to be.

Don't try to go it alone. Seek help if you need it. A few counseling sessions might be just the "umph" you need to change a trying situation into triumph. Then you and your "pardner" will discover happier trails as you ride into the sunset together.

# PART II

# Bettering Your Situation

❀

*In trying times, don't stop trying.*
—AUTHOR UNKNOWN

# 4

# He Drives Me Crazy

@/@

*I love being married. It's so great to find the one special*
*person you want to annoy for the rest of your life.*
—RITA RUDNER

Once you've agreed to accept the changes that an at-home
spouse brings and have begun to form a partnership with
him, you're ready for the next step—Bettering.

Bettering means looking at the problems you face and
deciding how to fix them.

Of course, you can't fix a problem if you don't know what
it is. So at this point you need to ask yourself what it is about
your present situation that really bothers you.

"My spouse" is not an acceptable answer. You need to be
more specific. Besides, we've already established the shortage
of good fairies with magic wands for hire.

Chances are that it's not your spouse you're unhappy
with—but his habits, or the fact that he's around all day. Some

wives feel a bit like Mary of nursery rhyme fame, whose lamb insisted on following her wherever she would go. As one woman complained to me, "It's like having a two-year-old around again. He follows me everywhere, asking, 'Whatcha doing? Where ya going?'"

Her solution is finding projects to keep her husband busy—roses that need trimming, a tricky doorknob that needs tweaking, an article on fly fishing that needs reading. These things buy her a little quiet time and satisfy her husband, who probably isn't happy in his role as her shadow anyway. Perhaps he's feeling lost in his new surroundings and needs help finding his place. As one observant person said, "A man's retirement is a wife's full-time job."

Once you determine what's really bothering you, make a list of the problems. Then choose two or three that you consider top priority and work on those.

What about the others? Try to ignore them. Dr. James Dobson's child-rearing advice applies to spouses as well: "Choose your battles carefully." Don't let an insignificant irritation ruin your relationship with your husband. As Texas Bix Bender reminds us in *Don't Squat with Yer Spurs On!*, "Solvin' problems is like throwin' cattle. Dig your heels in on the big ones, and catch the little ones 'round the neck."[1]

So what are some of your big ones?

Here's a list of the complaints I hear most often. Note that many couples attend my workshops, so some of these concerns come from husbands as well as wives:

- Lack of privacy
- Annoying habits
- Grocery shopping
- Upset routines
- Spousal inquisition
- Telephone

- Television
- Thermostat

Do any of these ring a bell? Let's look at some of these issues and possible solutions.

## This Little Hubby Went to Market

When Karl Malden warned in those TV ads, "Don't leave home without it," he wasn't referring to your mate. If you're like many wives I've met, leave your husband at home when you head for the grocery store.

Some couples actually enjoy shopping together. But most of the women I've talked to place grocery shopping with their spouses high on their list of complaints. Personally, I've seldom seen a cheerful couple perusing the produce aisles or strolling hand in hand through the checkout line. What I *have* witnessed are scenes like these:

> *Wife*: Put that box of Super Sugary Yum Yums back! I have a coupon for Lowfat Yucky Yum Yums. I swear, I can't take you anywhere.
>
> *Husband*: Stop wandering around! We need to have a plan. It would be more efficient to start over in produce and make our way to dairy.
>
> *Wife*: What did you do with the coupons? I gave them to you just as we were leaving the house. I ask you to do one little thing, and you can't get it right!
>
> *Husband*: How much longer is this going to take? If you'd made a list like I told you, we would have been out of here by now.
>
> *Wife*: Why are you going down that aisle? I got everything on our list. We don't need anything else. Get in line right now!

*Husband*: Why did you pick this line? I told you
the other one was faster. Look at that! If we'd been
behind that lady in the other line, it would be our
turn now.

What is it about shopping for groceries that turns so many
polite, devoted couples into disrespectful ogres? Is it something in the air ducts? Perhaps an undiscovered virus similar
to Legionnaire's disease? If so, I have a name for it: the Bick-
ering Bug. If you want to avoid the bug, try to talk your
spouse into staying home. If he insists on coming along,
divide up your list and agree to meet at the checkstand. And
good luck deciding which stand!

Another option is to send your husband to the store for
you. This is your chance to grab a moment to yourself, perhaps to relax in a bubble bath or read a few chapters in that
novel you've been trying to finish.

You may, however, have to pay for those few moments of
freedom by preparing a grocery list for your husband. This is
not as easy as it sounds, especially with all the choices in the
supermarket. Not long ago you could send your spouse to the
store for a loaf of bread, a dozen eggs, and a quart of milk with
nary a worry. Today your husband may feel compelled to call
from Aisle 15 on his cell phone to ask, "Do you want white,
French, sourdough, whole wheat, or sprouted grain? And
how many grains—five, seven, eight? Do you want the day-
old bread? Why not? It's a better buy, and the bread is gonna
get old anyway. . . . About that milk, do you want whole, low-
fat, one percent, two percent, lactose free, buttermilk? Should
I get the gallon instead of the quart? It's a better buy. . . . When
you said a dozen eggs, did you really mean a dozen? They're
running a special on a two-dozen carton. Some of the eggs are
cracked, but they're going to get cracked anyway."

In our house, my husband usually makes the supermarket runs. He grew up in the grocery business, replenishing shelves for his father's chain of markets and later managing a few stores. He enjoys the sight of a well-stocked shelf, and can get downright passionate over an attractive end display. I don't want to deprive him of such pleasures, so I let him do the shopping—even though preparing a list for him is nerve-wracking.

When indicating the size of can I need, I usually write down "small," "medium," or "large." To the untrained eye, those would appear to be apt descriptions. But to those in the know (such as those who spent their childhoods stocking shelves), canned goods are a number 2, a 2 1/2, or a 303. This is all too confusing for me, so I try not to be picky about the size of items on my list. If Ken comes home with a gigantic bottle of catsup that won't fit in the refrigerator door, I just turn that baby on its side and shove it onto a shelf. Then I shut the door—and my mouth.

## E.T., Phone at Home

Many women complain that they don't feel free to chat on the phone with their friends the way they did before their husbands started hanging around all day. Men, on the other hand, maintain that the phone was not designed for chatting. Take my husband, for example. He believes that the proper way to use the phone is to "state your business, conclude your business, and hang up." Apparently anything else you say on the phone is pure gossip and a waste of time. In some cases this may be true, but I feel it's perfectly acceptable to call a friend to inquire, "How are you?" even if she has not been suffering from the sniffles or had major surgery.

Differences in opinion between men and women over

phone use has a lot to do with the fact that men tend to value productivity, while women value relationships. When Ken tells me I could accomplish more if I didn't talk on the phone so much, I remind him that I *am* accomplishing something—I'm strengthening relationships with my friends.

Out of consideration for my husband, however, I try to limit my phone calls—or make them when he's not home. I've found I can still keep in touch with friends and family by doing most of my chatting when Ken's running errands or jogging.

Even if your husband doesn't object to your phone time, you may face the privacy issue. "He is always hanging around, listening to every word I say," one frustrated wife told me, "and afterwards he wants to know what the other person said."

One approach to solving this problem is to move out of earshot, preferably to another room with the door shut. As long as you don't spend the entire day in there, you probably won't hurt his feelings. Or you could simply adopt the attitude of the woman who told me she's amused by her husband's nosiness, and doesn't have a problem with it.

Another frequent complaint I hear from women is that while they're on the phone, their husbands coach from the sidelines. "Tell her we got her letter," he says. "Ask her if she wants me to send some more jokes. Tell her that joke I told you the other day. Is she laughing?"

One woman deals with this by offering the phone to her husband and calmly saying, "Here, you tell her yourself." That remark generally sends him scurrying from the room. And it sounds so much nicer than "Go away!"

Some women complain that their phone lines are tied up by their husbands, who spend hours on the Internet. If this is a problem for you, suggest to your spouse that he either limit his time at the computer or add a line dedicated to Internet access. (You'll probably have more success getting him to agree to the latter.)

If your husband works from home, it's best to have two phone lines—a private one and a business one. Otherwise you may never be able to use the phone for fear that your husband will miss an important call. And Call Waiting is not an acceptable substitute for a second line. It just doesn't sound professional to tell your spouse's client, "Hang on, I'm on the line with Jane. As soon as she finishes telling me about her gall bladder surgery, I'll switch you over to my husband."

One more thought on telephone etiquette: Consider your priorities. If a friend calls when you and your husband are engaged in conversation or an activity, ask her to call you back. Your husband needs to know that he is valued as much as your friend is. Friends may need to be reminded that our husbands are now home during the day. Let the caller know in a gentle, kind way if it's not a convenient time to talk.

## Those Nasty Habits

What's your husband's most annoying habit? Is it the way he slurps his cereal or cracks his knuckles? Is it the way he *breathes*, as one woman actually complained?

The longer you've been married, the longer your list of pet peeves is bound to be. It's not so much that your spouse has added more bad habits over the years, but simply that the ones which you could easily put up with in the early days of your marriage have gradually eaten away at your nerves. Now they've reached that really tender spot that makes you yell "Ouch!"—and the honeymoon Novocain has worn off.

Now that your husband is home 24/7, you get a chance to see those irritating habits displayed frequently—and feel the pain more sharply. You fear you can no longer be responsible for your actions if he leaves those cracker crumbs in the sink one more time!

How can you deal with irritating habits? Try speaking the truth—in love (Ephesians 4:15). Point out to your husband, in a calm voice and preferably with a sense of humor, that what he is doing really bugs you. Perhaps he'll make an effort to change his ways. Old habits are very hard to break, though, so don't expect miracles.

Once the behavior has been named, you can express your feelings the next time he repeats it. It's far better to say, "You are driving me crazy again," than to actually be driven crazy by holding in the anger.

Meanwhile, try to admit that you may have irritating habits yourself. Perhaps if you ask your spouse to identify your little quirks and then spend time working on those, you won't keep concentrating on his.

If this approach doesn't work, consider wearing a "What Would Jesus Do?" bracelet. The bracelet itself might not be an ideal choice for your jewelry collection, but its motto is well worth remembering—especially at stressful moments. I've been thinking about printing "What Would Jesus Do?" on a sticky note and attaching it to our bathroom mirror. Then the next time I find the capless tube of toothpaste lying in a pool of sticky, cool mint gel, I might not lose *my* cool.

Don't forget to pray for your husband. Ask for patience. Take your complaints to the Lord and leave them there. Trust Him to make things better between the two of you.

It might also help to write a list of things that are driving you up the wall. When you look at it, you'll see how insignificant most of the items are. True, fleas and ants are irritating despite their tiny size. But we need to develop a new attitude about this small stuff, heeding the title of Richard Carlson's book *Don't Sweat the Small Stuff… and It's All Small Stuff.* Let's stop sweating and start counting to 10.

Once we've calmed down, we can start developing compassion for our mates—in spite of their irritating habits. (This sounds like something Jesus would do, doesn't it?) As author Claudia Arp notes, it helps to remember that we are to "cleave" (Genesis 2:24, King James Version) to our spouses for life. "Cleaving," writes Claudia, "means sticking together no matter what and giving each other permission to be less than perfect." (This probably includes partaking of one's cereal in a less than perfect way.) She suggests that we lighten up. "There are times in marriage where you'll either laugh or cry. Dave and I have decided if at all possible, we'll choose laughter over tears."[2]

I opt for laughter—and I hope you do, too.

## Don't Touch That Button

Let's look at two final areas where control battles are waged daily between at-home spouses—television viewing and thermostat settings.

Many couples have different tastes when it comes to TV programs. The obvious solution is to purchase a second television set.

I wouldn't recommend that for newlyweds. But seasoned couples who find themselves together 24 hours a day can afford to spend a little time apart. Television viewing is one area where compromising seldom works; it's unrealistic to expect an ESPN fan to convert a Food Network buff, or vice versa.

If buying a second television set isn't possible, try watching one show while taping another. Unfortunately, my husband and I can't agree on who gets to see the live production and who has to wait to view the tape. That's why we have "his" and "her" TV sets—one upstairs, one downstairs. (I take the upstairs because it's so much warmer up there!)

Speaking of temperature, thermostats are a problem for an amazing number of at-home couples. You and your mate may be a perfect match, but chances are that your metabolisms are not. Control of the thermostat appears to be edging out the battle over the TV remote when it comes to the major source of arguments among spouses. One mate typically shivers while the other swelters, and shouts of "Who messed with the thermostat?" echo off the walls.

At our house, it is considered a federal crime to move the thermostat needle more than one notch at a time. Just to be seen lurking near the thermostat is cause for suspicion. Short of installing a security camera, I don't have a solution for this problem.

It would seem logical to keep the temperature at a low setting and let the cold-blooded ones grab a sweater and pile on the blankets. The less logical alternative would be to hitch it up to 80 degrees and let warm-blooded family members pass out from the heat. But when I voiced my opinion at a recent workshop, I was bombarded with hisses. I had unknowingly stumbled into a pit of cold-blooded creatures whose cry was, "Take it off, take it off," rather than, "Pile it on."

Because of this reaction, I no longer offer solutions. Instead, I ask for suggestions. One woman volunteered her husband's unusual remedy: "He thinks I should go in for a blood transfusion once a month." Thin-blooded people, take note!

The thermostat war will continue to rage for a long time. This is one area in which your compromising skills will be put to the test.

## The Choice Is Yours

When it comes to dealing with the things about our at-home

husbands that drive us crazy, it pays to keep things in perspective. Commentator Andy Rooney might have had that in
mind when he wrote these words in a list called "What I've
Learned":

> I've learned . . . that being kind is more impor-
> tant than being right.
> I've learned . . . that when you harbor bitterness,
> happiness will dock elsewhere.
> I've learned . . . that one should keep his words
> both soft and tender, because tomorrow you may
> have to eat them.
> I've learned . . . that I can't choose how I feel, but
> I can choose what I do.

We can't help it if our husbands get on our nerves at
times. But we can help what we do with our angry feelings.
We can choose to count to ten, shoot off a prayer for patience,
or laugh it off.

I think I'll go for all three.

# 5

# I Want to Be Alone

@@

*Constant togetherness is fine,*
*but only if you are Siamese twins.*
—VICTORIA BILLINGS

Lack of privacy is such a big concern for most women in my
seminars that I've considered selling "Do Not Disturb" door
hangers. I could probably make a fortune. It's not that these
women intend to do anything illegal or immoral behind their
closed doors; they just want a spouse-free zone where they
can relax.

"Just once, I would like to be able to lie on my bed in the
middle of the day, without worrying that my husband will
think I've had a heart attack and call the paramedics,"
lamented one beleaguered wife.

She no doubt needed what author Sarah Ban Breathnach
claims all women need and desire—a nap.

The general consensus among women I've talked to is that
when the husband is around, the wife has no time to gather

her thoughts. Her spouse is either constantly engaging her in conversation, or in one of his projects. His idea is to be "productive" at all times. Men don't seem to realize that moments spent in quiet thought, or even daydreaming, are usually productive for women. That's where some of their most creative ideas are born.

To obtain this much-needed quiet time, it isn't always necessary to hang a "Do Not Disturb" sign on your door. It just requires the courage to be honest with your mate. Let him know that your wanting to be alone is not a reflection on him, but simply a way to recharge your batteries. (References to electrical sources seem to work well with men.)

If your husband doesn't honor your request, it might be necessary to close your door to signal that you mean business. Of course, this does not always work. Remember Ken knocking on my office door? Some women discover the only way they can find any privacy is to leave the house and stake out a quiet place in the library or park.

The desire for a quiet spot of your own is perfectly natural; you don't have to feel guilty. Teenagers seek refuge in their bedrooms; younger children carve out a spot on the couch or the living room floor. When my five-year-old grandson, Aaron, comes to visit, he drags a futon pad into the living room and whips it into a tent or cave. Even our cat has her hiding spot under the daybed in our guest room.

Your husband probably has his favorite easy chair, too. Everyone deserves a place to go when the need for privacy arrives.

## Hiding from the Trash Inspector

Some of us aren't so much concerned with a place to hide ourselves; we're looking for a place to hide our trash. If your husband fancies himself a garbage inspector, a secret trash pile is high on your list of privacy needs.

Were my husband to discover the amount of food I have allowed to linger in our refrigerator until it's become an unrecognizable blob of fuzz, he would be horrified. Leftovers are apparently meant to be eaten, but I find that they make an excellent breeding ground for mold. I may not have a green thumb when it comes to roses or azaleas, but I'm an expert at cultivating spores. I don't even need a Petri dish; a Pyrex dish will work just fine.

So how do I hide the evidence and avoid the "waste not, want not" lecture I deserve? I wrap up the UFOs (Unidentifiable Food Objects) in aluminum foil and hide them in the back of my freezer until I find an opportune time to dispose of them. My husband's annual visit to his Texas relatives has become my traditional garbage-purging period. Of course, a year's supply of UFOs can really add up; I'm sure my neighbors must wonder why we seem to have the most trash cans on our curb when I'm the only one home!

My friend Susan's biggest trash disposal problem isn't rotten garbage but ratty underwear. She called me recently to describe the scene when her husband, Ed, discovered a pair of his old, holey underwear in the laundry room's wastebasket.

"Now mind you," she explained to me, "the waistband on this baby had totally lost its elasticity, and the shorts were only hanging on to it by a few threads. Yet Ed was livid at the thought of his 'perfectly good' pair of Jockey shorts being discarded. He rushed into the kitchen where I was preparing dinner and started waving his shorts about as if they were a football pennant. But instead of cheering he was screeching, 'How did these get into the wastebasket?'"

Susan tried to explain to her husband that she'd purchased a new package of underwear and was rotating them into his supply when she'd come across some that were obviously past their prime. But Ed would have none of it. "He just kept twirling those old shorts around, while declaring that he and he alone would be the one to decide if the elastic band had sufficient elasticity remaining."

Susan finally gave in and returned the old shorts to his drawer. But a week later, only minutes before the scheduled arrival of the garbage truck, she called to tell me she was going to be rid of that old pair of shorts once and for all (unless the truck arrived late and her mate returned early from a game of golf)! Susan's theory of trash disposal now involves waiting until trash day to throw anything out. She's counting on her husband not having enough time to rummage through the cans and pull stuff out.

## Too Close for Comfort

Another lack-of-privacy complaint I frequently hear is, "We keep bumping into each other all day." When a fellow Bible study member arrived late one morning, she blamed it on her husband's habit of fixing breakfast at the very moment she's trying to whip up something for herself.

"He knows this is my Bible study day and I have to get an early start," she lamented. "He has all morning to mess around in the kitchen, so why can't he wait until I leave to start his meal?"

No one had an answer for that. Some women were in awe, however, over the fact that her husband made his own breakfast.

Ken and I often find ourselves in the midst of physical comedy as we try to maneuver our way around the kitchen without causing serious bodily harm to each other, especially in the morning. He reaches for a glass in the cabinet above me as I root through a bottom drawer in search of a pan, and when I stand up—WHAM! His cabinet door and my head meet. If he bends over to grab the waffle iron from the bottom cabinet just as I back away from the oven door with a hot tray of biscuits, our backsides collide and he lands in the cabinet among the pots and pans.

If I were a morning person, I suppose I could laugh at our antics. But I'm not. Since I'm not exactly pleasant company till the fog lifts from my brain, we're toying with the idea of initiating first and second seatings for breakfast. You and your mate might also want to give each other a wider berth if your kitchen seems to have shrunk since your husband came home. If you find yourself tripping over him in other rooms as well, look for patterns and avoid areas where you know he'll be at certain times.

Here's another idea: If you have a spare bedroom, consider converting it into a den for your husband. If you have a guest bath, try making it his or yours. My husband and I made this move gradually. At first Ken moved his toothbrush and toothpaste into the guest bathroom to keep from disturbing me when he began his day at the crack of dawn. His new arrangement worked so well that he decided to shave in that bathroom, too. After a while he thought of that bath as his, and so did I.

## Girl Interrupted

Some wives wish for privacy because their at-home husbands are always interrupting them. These women often hear things like, "Honey, come outside for a minute. I want to show you this fascinating weed in our garden. You won't believe how big it is!"

If you have this kind of husband, he might invite you to

accompany him to the building supply store to check out a display of nails. To entice you to join him in this exciting adventure, he may add, "You won't believe how many they have!" How could you possibly pass up such an offer?

If your husband is retired, he may be interrupting because he's lonely and lost now that he has no job to go to every day. You, on the other hand, have plenty to do. Still, it's kindest to accompany him on some of his adventures, especially close-by ones—like seeing that garden weed.

That doesn't mean your routines aren't important, however, especially when your life is undergoing so many changes. Let your mate know—gently—that you can't always drop everything and run off with him on his madcap exploits, no matter how enticing they might be.

Help him establish his own routines, too. Men who are used to knowing exactly what's expected of them each day in the workplace don't always know how to react to the freedom of being at home. If your mate needs goals to get him through the day, help him create a few. They could be as simple as taking a walk around the block or as complex as upgrading your computer's system software. Maybe he'll want to take up my husband's favorite pastime, emptying wastebaskets and filling ice trays!

Don't hand your spouse a "Honey Do" list of chores, though. My neighbor once confessed to me that his wife's long assignment list sent him back to the workplace after an early retirement. He probably felt like the guy who defined leisure time as "any time your wife can't find you."

Interruptions will become less frequent as your spouse establishes meaningful routines, especially those that take him out of the house and into the satisfying world of volunteer work. You'll find more on this subject in chapter 9.

## The Spousal Inquisition

Although not quite as severe as the Spanish Inquisition, the Spousal Inquisition can be very uncomfortable for wives who need privacy.

"Where are you going? Why are you going there? When will you be back? What shall I tell someone if they phone for you?" These are the questions my husband blurts out when he sees me grab my car keys.

In the beginning, I was incensed over his questions. After all, I was an adult, not a teenager. I didn't need permission to take the car. There was no curfew hanging over my head and no reason to give an accounting of my whereabouts.

As far as I was concerned, my husband's actions signaled a battle for control, and I was not going to relinquish my independence. I refused to answer his questions. I might tell him where I was going, but I wouldn't commit to a time of return. And I certainly didn't want to leave a phone number where I could be reached.

One day, though, a man at one of my seminars changed my thinking. Richard had been retired for only a few months. As we discussed the Spousal Inquisition problem, his wife, June, complained that she'd recently returned late from a church meeting only to discover that her husband had gone out looking for her. "Why would he do that?" she asked. She was a perfectly capable adult, not some wayward, young daughter.

"Because I was worried about her," Richard explained to our class. "I thought she might have had a flat tire, or been in an accident." A former police officer, Richard was well aware of the possibilities.

His explanation sounded very familiar. Just a few weeks

before, Ken had been upset with me when I'd returned from a meeting much later than he'd expected.

"What difference does it make what time I get back?" I'd yelled.

"Because I thought something might have happened to you!" he'd yelled back.

Somewhere underneath all that yelling had lurked caring spouses who were misinterpreting each other's actions. Instead of being grateful that Ken cared enough to worry about me, I had resented his intrusion. I hadn't understood that his anger over my tardiness represented concern, not control.

Listening to Richard plead his case at the workshop, however, brought the point home. Even though I'd insisted I wasn't a teenager, I'd been acting like one.

Would it have hurt me to take a moment to call and let Ken know that I was going to be late? Of course not. I needed to change my attitude. Once I started thinking of "reporting in" as an act of respect rather than a humiliating sign of weakness, it was easy to honor Ken's request to call if I was delayed.

I also started to realize that a husband who has worked all his life as an accountant would naturally request an accounting of my actions. He wanted to know the facts so he could feel more secure.

As Ken and I discussed this, he admitted that it bothered him when someone called for me and he was unable to tell them when I'd be back. He felt obligated to act as my personal secretary, and didn't want to be a dumb one—or to give out false information. I reassured him that I didn't expect him to be my secretary, and in fact I preferred he not take on that role.

I also reminded him that before he started working from home, I spent many hours on the road. Had he been sitting at his office desk, worrying about me? Of course not. He'd known that I had a cell phone, I was enrolled in an roadside assistance plan, and there was no shortage of highway patrolmen in our area. Those things were still true.

Now when I leave the house I usually say something like, "I'm off to Sally's. We're going to lunch and then may do some shopping, so I don't know for sure where I'll be or when I'll be home. But I probably won't be gone for more than two or three hours."

We've come a long way in our understanding of each other. Ken has grown pretty comfortable with my excursions, and is less likely to ask for my itinerary or to dial 911 when I'm running late. By the same token, I'm far more willing to share information about my whereabouts, and no longer yearn to sneak out of the house undetected.

If your husband worries about you when you're away, remind him of this old saying: "Worry is like a rocking chair; it gives you something to do, but it doesn't get you anywhere." Be grateful for your husband's concern, but don't hesitate to head out the door. Be patient, be gentle, and . . . be gone!

## Prayer Changes Things

No matter what kind of privacy issues you face, remember the power of prayer.

Now more than ever you need the strength and peace that come from spending time alone with the Lord. Pray not just for yourself, but for your husband as well. This is especially important when you're upset with him. Stormie Omartian, in her book *The Power of a Praying Wife*, points out that seeing your husband through God's eyes—as His child—can be a great revelation. "If someone called and asked you to pray for his or her son, you would do it, wouldn't you? Well, God is asking."[1]

She goes on to explain, "Nagging doesn't work! Criticizing doesn't work. Sometimes just plain talk doesn't accomplish anything either. I've found that prayer is the only thing that always works."[2]

The reason for this is simple. When you pray, you're dealing with the Creator of the universe. That sobering thought can help you develop the right attitude toward having a spouse in the house.

# 6

# Failures to Communicate

❦

*The best way to get the last word is to apologize.*
—AUTHOR UNKNOWN

In real estate it's "location, location, location." In marriage, it's "communication, communication, communication."

Take the lady whose husband asked her what she'd like for her birthday.

"I'd love to be seven again," she replied.

So on the morning of her birthday, hubby got her up bright and early and dragged her to an amusement park. Five hours later, after he'd put her on every ride from the Death Slide to the Screaming Loop, she staggered out of the park—head reeling and stomach upside-down.

Immediately she was whisked to McDonald's for a Happy

Meal and chocolate shake. Then it was off to an animated movie—with nachos, popcorn, and candy.

Finally the poor woman wobbled home with her husband and collapsed into bed. He leaned over and lovingly asked, "Well, Dear, what was it like being seven again?"

She opened one eye. "I meant my dress size," she said wearily.

Now *there's* a failure to communicate.

Lack of communication skills is probably the biggest issue in most marriages, and one which seems to get worse when both spouses are home. In fact, it lurks behind most of the problems we've discussed so far.

How often do you *really* talk with your spouse about meaningful matters? Daily? Weekly? Monthly? As the old joke puts it, if you see two people eating dinner together at a restaurant and they're silent, you can be sure they're married.

A recent sitcom got it right. A husband and wife finally got away from their kids for a quiet dinner at an expensive restaurant, only to find they had nothing to talk about. They spent the entire evening discussing the quality of the bread and butter. When they ran out of bread, a look of horror passed across the husband's face. He and his wife immediately leaped to their feet to signal the waiter for more bread!

One national study reported the amazing finding that married couples talk to each other—really talk to each other about something meaningful—for only 17 minutes a month.[1]

As shocking as that finding is, it's easy to see how this can happen in a busy family when husband and wife are separated by distance during the day. When night falls, they're probably both too weary to manage much more than, "Did you set the alarm?" or, "Do I have a clean shirt for tomorrow?" Even these questions might prompt an argument rather than a fascinating conversation—especially if the answer to either is no.

Retired and work-at-home couples don't have physical separation as an excuse for poor communication. Yet many of them have trouble finding something to say to each other.

Perhaps they mistakenly believe it's worth talking only if they have something "profound" to talk about. But as author Shelby Hearon writes, "There is nothing too trivial to broach our spouse about and therefore nothing too serious either." She remembers calling her husband to report seeing a starling in their birdbath. This observation triggered memories that led to a confession of childhood disappointments. Her husband mentioned his sore toe, which opened the door to revealing his deep anxieties about growing old and losing the ability to walk. Eventually they moved from this serious discussion of their own mortality back to more trivial matters. As Hearon points out, this kind of discourse isn't possible if most of your hours become "not important enough" or "too serious" to trouble your spouse about.[2]

## Lend Me Your Ears

Just agreeing to converse with your spouse on a daily basis doesn't necessarily mean you'll be communicating, of course. The process involves not only talking—but listening.

We all need someone to listen to us. I was reminded of this recently while browsing in a large bookstore. All the store's information booths contained computers which customers were supposed to access, but I wanted something more low-tech. To my relief, I spotted a human being standing behind a counter across the room. I hurried over to ask him for help in locating a book, but stopped short when I saw this sign on the counter: *Dear Customer, As of February 19, we will be unable to provide you with listening on demand. We apologize for any inconvenience.*

Did this mean I had to make an appointment to talk to the clerk? What on earth was this world coming to? My face must have registered my confusion, because the young man asked, "Ma'am, are you okay? Can I help you with something?"

"Well, I'm not sure. I don't have an appointment, but I was wondering if you had a certain book."

It was his turn to be confused. "An appointment? What are you talking about?" I pointed to the sign, but he still seemed bewildered. "Did you want to listen to a CD?" he asked.

That's when I learned that "listening on demand" means previewing a tape or CD before purchasing it. Boy, did I feel foolish (and out of the loop)!

It can be tempting to try the same thing with our at-home husbands. Weary of listening, we may want to make a copy of that sign and hang it around our necks—letting them know we're no longer available for "listening on demand."

The truth is, most of us will never do this. As women, we seem born to listen. It's what we do. It's our job and we take it seriously. We train to become better listeners by reading books on the subject. We ask for advice from friends, and listen to what they tell us.

We also realize that listening doesn't always require a response. In fact, the ability to keep your ears open and your mouth closed is usually the sign of a good listener. As author Susan Lenzkes points out, "It's good to remember that 'listen' and 'silent' are made of the same six letters."[3]

Many men, on the other hand, seem to think that when a woman mentions a concern to them, it's because she wants them to do something about it. They can't seem to comprehend the notion of "venting." They don't realize that all we need is a sympathetic hug or a simple "I understand" (even if they don't)! I know one clever woman who begins conversations with her husband by saying, "Take off your fix-it hat." When he hears those words, he knows that nothing is required of him but to listen—silently listen.

## Speaking Your Husband's Language

No wonder communication often breaks down in Spouse-in-the-House marriages. Men and women seem to be speaking different languages.

Just listen to the way author Lysa TerKeurst and her husband tended to converse in the early days of their wedded bliss:

> *Lysa*: Hi, honey, how was your day?
> *Art*: Good.
> *Lysa*: Mine too. I took Hope and Ashley for their well checkups today. (Meaning I took the girls to the doctor not because they were sick but because it was time for their annual physicals.)
> *Art*: (Silently wondering what our water well needed to be checked for and how our daughters fit into the same sentence.)
> *Lysa*: (Feeling a little frustrated at his silence, which I interpret as a lack of caring.) And they were fine . . . (thinking: *Not that you seem to care*.)[4]

So how can you talk to your at-home husband in a language he understands? Here are some suggestions.

1. *Beware of blaming.* Many men assume that when a woman wants to talk to him about her problems, it's because she is blaming him for them. If that's not the case, the woman

needs to let him know. Dr. John Gray, author of *Men Are from Mars, Women Are from Venus*, suggests that wives preface their conversations with these magic words: "It's not your fault, but . . ."[5]

On the other hand, if the husband *is* to blame for a problem and the wife is upset, Dr. Gray recommends that she share her anger with someone else first—a friend, perhaps. "Confront him only after you have cooled off and can be more supportive when talking to him," Gray advises.[6]

2. *Remember that men tend to deal with one issue at a time.* Bill and Pam Farrel, Christian co-founders of Masterful Living, an organization that provides practical insights for married couples, explain it this way in their book *Men Are Like Waffles, Women Are Like Spaghetti*:

"If you look at a waffle, you see a collection of boxes separated by walls. The boxes are all separate from each other and make convenient holding places. That is typically how a man processes life. Our thinking is divided up into boxes that have room for one issue and one issue only."[7]

This compartmentalizing tendency makes men problem solvers, according to the Farrels. "They enter a box, size up the problem and formulate a solution."[8]

Women, on the other hand, are like pasta noodles that touch one another and everything else on their plates. Thus, they are the spaghetti. The Farrels believe "women are in pursuit of connecting life together. Women consistently sense the need to talk things through. In conversation she can link together the logical, emotional, and spiritual aspects of the issue."[9]

Trouble comes when a poor husband tries to jump from box to box to keep up with his wife's conversation. Remember Lysa TerKeurst's chat with her spouse about their daughters' "well checkups"? From that point on, things just got more confusing for Art:

> *Lysa*: Anyhow (obviously annoyed), on my way to the doctor's office I was driving down Providence Road, and I noticed that all the trees had black tape wrapped around them. It appears to be some sort of pest control treatment. Do you think our trees could be in danger of these bugs? Because if so, I think I'd like to try this tape stuff, which is probably a lot safer than spraying chemicals that could harm the children. You know, I just don't think our government is doing enough to protect our children from dangerous pesticides. So, do you think I should spend extra money at the grocery store for organic produce? If so, I'll need you to add some money to my grocery budget.
>
> *Art*: (Wondering how the well, our daughters, the trees on Providence Road, and the government's stand on pesticides could end in a request to spend more money. He decides to play it safe.) I don't know, honey; I'll have to think about it.
>
> *Lysa*: (Astonished at his lack of concern for our family's health, begins to cry.) You'll have to think about what? We are talking about our daughters' lives here and all you can say is you'll think about it!
>
> *Art*: (Baffled, still not understanding how any of this relates to our daughters' lives but clearly understanding I'm asking for more money again.) Why are you so emotional, and why are you always nagging me for more money? (He realizes he shouldn't have said nagging, remembering he got something thrown

at him the last time he used that word. He regrets his choice of words and ducks just in case.)

*Lysa*: Nagging? You call caring for our children *nagging*? You are so insensitive . . . you're impossible. You're not worth wasting any more of my breath! (Stomp, stomp, stomp, slam.)

*Art: Women! What's the deal? And what did she ever say was wrong with our well?*[10]

To make it easier for *your* spouse to listen, try to address one subject at a time.

3. *Accept the differences in the way you communicate.* As the Farrels put it, "Two guitar players will sound a little different when they are playing the same song, and two drivers will have different styles of driving even though they arrive at the same destination."[11]

One lady in my seminar, married for 55 years, had the best solution. "Why can't you just sit down and talk to your husband and hear each other out?" she asked. "It doesn't matter if you are coming from different views." Her husband nodded in agreement. Perhaps it's this willingness to "hear each other out" that has kept that couple together all these years.

4. *Watch your timing.* In her book *Help Me, I'm Married!*, Joyce Meyer suggests that people often don't communicate well because of poor timing and insensitivity to God's leading. She advises waiting until you sense the presence of God preparing the heart of the person with whom you need to communicate.[12]

"Timing is extremely important in good communication," she writes. "If you start talking to someone who sighs and looks away it is fair to assume they don't want to hear what you have to say or they are too distracted to pay attention to you at that time. We can cause ourselves trouble by not picking the right time to speak."[13]

Referring to Ecclesiastes 3:7, which says there is a time to speak and a time to be silent, Meyer notes that there's a time to talk about a problem and a time to leave it alone. "That doesn't mean that you should never talk about it," she explains, "but you should look for the right time to discuss the topic on your heart if you want it to be received with a fair evaluation."[14]

## Check Your Conversational Style

Do you and your at-home husband speak the same language, but still get your signals crossed? Perhaps you have different conversational styles.

In their book *The Language of Love*, Gary Smalley and John Trent describe "Head Talk" or "Fact Talk" and "Heart Talk" or "Feeling Talk." Women, they explain, speak a language of the heart. They are comfortable with both facts and feelings, while men desire to keep their feelings bottled up and want to deal with facts like box scores and batting average.[15]

As for my husband and me, his desire for Head Talk prompts him to insist that I get to the bottom line when I'm relating an event to him. He wants "just the facts, Ma'am." As a Heart Talker, I want to describe the things that touched me—like what everyone wore and who said what to whom.

This is the way our conversation usually goes when I return from my seminars:

> *Ken:* How did your talk go?
> *Me:* Great! I have to tell you about this one lady. She was dressed in this really sharp-looking outfit—I think it was a Liz Claiborne, but it might have been

an Alfred Dunner. Anyway, you won't believe this funny story she told about—

    *Ken:* (cutting me off) How many people were there?

    *Me:* I don't know, but let me tell you about—

    *Ken:* What do you mean, you don't know? How many seats did the room hold?

    *Me:* (annoyed at his interruptions) How should I know?

    *Ken:* Well, how many rows were there?

    *Me:* (extremely annoyed) Why would I know that? And why on earth does it matter, anyway?

    *Ken:* If you knew how many rows there were, you could count the number of seats in each row and then multiply that number to know how many people were in attendance.

Evidently when my husband looks out upon an audience, he sees seats to be counted. I see outfits to be admired and stories to be heard.

Dr. Deborah Tannen, professor of linguistics at Georgetown University, illustrates another way conversational styles can clash. She tells the story of a couple out for a drive. The wife asks if her husband would like to stop for refreshments. He answers truthfully, "No."

They continue driving. When they arrive home, the husband is puzzled by his wife's silent treatment. *What could I possibly have done to deserve her anger?* he wonders.[16]

"In understanding what went wrong," Dr. Tannen concludes, "the husband should realize that when she asks what he would like, she is not asking an information question, but rather starting a negotiation about what both would like. For her part however, the woman must understand that when a man says 'No,' it is not meant as a non-negotiable demand. In this case it was simply a truthful answer to her question, 'Do *you* want to stop?' "[17]

When I talked about this in a seminar, one man raised his hand and asked, "So, basically, we men are expected to be mind readers?"

"Yes!" every woman in the room shouted back.

Such an expectation is unfair to our poor husbands, of course. We need to say what we mean, and mean what we say. In this case, the woman should have said, "I want to stop for something to eat. Do you?"

## Dealing with Personality Conflicts

For some at-home couples, it's not different planets or different phrasings that short-circuit communication. It's different personalities.

"Opposites attract, but like is easier to be married to," said Diana Douglas Darid. Those words ring true for Ken and me. He's an accountant and I'm a writer. We are a classic example of the left-brain (logical) vs. right-brain (random) syndrome. With such differences, it's easy to see why Ken and I have trouble communicating.

Short of a brain transplant, I didn't think we could solve this problem—until I attended Marita Littauer's seminar on personality styles. Her explanation of four basic temperaments opened my eyes to how I could approach Ken in a way that would meet the needs of his personality.

Ken's temperament is the Perfect Personality—analytical, conscientious, serious, and thoughtful. Perfect Personalities tend to marry Popular Personalities (like myself) for their outgoing nature and social skills—and soon attempt to quiet them and get them on schedule. Poor Ken. What an overwhelming challenge I must be!

As a Popular Personality, I am talkative, emotional, and spontaneous. I don't know how to be quiet. As for schedules, I can't tell you how many "day planners" my ever-hopeful husband has given me—and how many I've lost.

In spite of our differences, I'm learning to speak effectively with Ken. I "turn down the volume" when I talk to him. I try to ask, "When would be a good time for us to go out to dinner?" instead of surprising him with, "Here are the car keys. Let's go!" I'm also trying to respect his need for solitude—which means curbing my desire to talk all the time.

How about you? Are you and your husband unequally yoked when it comes to temperament? Here's a short overview of the four styles, based on material from *Personality Puzzle* by Florence Littauer and Marita Littauer.[18] See if you can spot yourself and your spouse.

POPULAR PERSONALITY (Talkers)
Talkative, bubbly, emotional, sincere, and curious.
*Desire:* To have fun.
*Emotional Needs:* Attention, affection, approval, acceptance.

POWERFUL PERSONALITY (Workers)
Strong-willed, dynamic, active, and decisive.
*Desire:* To have control.
*Emotional Needs:* Sense of obedience, and appreciation for accomplishments.

PERFECT PERSONALITY (Thinkers)
Analytical, conscientious, serious, and thoughtful.
*Desire:* To have it right.
*Emotional Needs:* Stability, space, silence, support.

PEACEFUL PERSONALITY (Watchers)
Easy-going, quiet, patient, and sympathetic.
*Desire:* To have peace.
*Emotional Needs:* Respect, understanding, feeling of worth.

Once you've identified your personality and that of your husband, consider the following ways to effectively communicate with him.

1. When talking to a spouse with a Peaceful Personality, approach him calmly. If you're a Popular Personality, slow your boisterous speech pattern down a few notches. If you're a Powerful Personality, back up a few paces to avoid an "in your face" attitude. No matter what your temperament, begin your conversation with a word of praise to boost your mate's sense of self-worth.

2. If your husband is a Powerful Personality, get to the point. This will take some practice for Popular Personalities, who tend to ramble. Peaceful Personalities need to be more forceful when requesting something of a Powerful Personality. Perfect Personalities should watch their tendency to point out flaws; give the Powerful Personality the recognition he craves. "I just don't know how you do all that you do!" is about the best thing you can say to a Powerful Personality, according to Marita.

3. When talking to a Popular Personality, laugh at his humor. Take an interest in his stories and give him your full attention. Powerfuls, who want to cut to the bottom line, need to practice patience; Peacefuls need to show some excitement (even if they don't feel it) when conversing with a Popular spouse. Perfect Personalities would do well to start the conversation with a compliment.

4. To communicate effectively with a Perfect Personality,

wait for the right moment. Ask, "Would this be a good time to talk?" and respect his answer. It's also a good idea to plan what you want to say before approaching him. I often present requests to my Perfect Personality spouse in the form of a proposal. I write out a concise list of my concerns and submit it to him. This "cuts to the chase" and allows Ken time to respond to my ideas. Perfects don't like to be put on the spot; they need time to reflect before making decisions. It's also wise to use as few words as possible. Otherwise your Perfect mate is liable to agree with Rodney Dangerfield, who lamented, "I haven't spoken to my wife in years. I didn't want to interrupt her."

These ideas should get you started on the road to better communication with a spouse whose personality differs from your own. After pondering your mate's emotional needs, you'll probably come up with original strategies, too.

No matter which differences may be causing a communication gap between you and your at-home husband—different planets, different phrasings, or different personalities —celebrate those differences. You may even find that your strengths can offset his weaknesses—and vice versa.

# 7

# Laughing Matters

@@

*Humor is to life what shock absorbers
are to automobiles.*
—AUTHOR UNKNOWN

Want to know the secret to a long and happy marriage? Fred, a retired military officer, offers this advice: "Never let your wife hear you whistling when you are packing."

Another husband, Ron, insists that the secret to his happy marriage to a woman named Sherry is three little words: "Yes, Sherry Dear."

What do these two men have in common? A great sense of humor—the *real* secret to a successful marriage. I predict both of these couples will have little trouble adjusting to being at home together. When I talk to couples who seem to be sailing smoothly through 24/7 togetherness, the first thing I notice is their ability to laugh at themselves.

With a sense of humor, you can weather the rough spots in any relationship. If you're a parent, you've probably already developed this survival skill. How can you *not* laugh when, on the one day that you let your son exchange his usually nutritious breakfast for a gooey, glazed donut and a cup of hot chocolate, his health teacher asks him to tell the class the ingredients of his morning meal? Nor can you stifle a chuckle when your four-year-old daughter finally gets her turn to say grace at your family's large Thanksgiving gathering and prays, "Thank you, Grace."

## Building Your Humor Muscles

How's *your* sense of humor? If the stresses of too much togetherness have made it hard to see what's funny about life, here are some simple ways to develop your humor muscles.

1. *Read, watch, and listen to humor.* Look for humor in your local newspaper. Start with the comics. If your paper carries it, pay close attention to "Pickles," which depicts the trials of seasoned spouses trying to cope with each other's foibles. The wife's beloved cat drives the husband crazy, and his beloved TV remote control often falls prey to the wife's sabotage. When you recognize yourself or your spouse in these day-to-day scenarios, you can't help but laugh.

Many magazines contain plenty of humor too, especially in their cartoons. That's where I found a cartoon in which Snow White vacuums the floor as the seven dwarfs trudge in line behind her. Snow White says, "I just wish you guys had given some thought to what you were going to do after you retired."

View a few TV comedies. Browse the humor section in bookstores or at your local library. Listen to comedy albums, like the classic routines of Bill Cosby and Bob Newhart. Comedians like these are adept at finding humor in the mundane and irritating—exactly the skill you need to develop!

2. *Spend time with children.* Kids are a great source of laughter. If you have children or grandchildren, you can probably think of a few cute witticisms they've uttered. If you don't have offspring, listen to your neighbors' kids. Or check out one of my favorite "out of the mouths of babes" stories:

> A three-year-old went with his dad to see a litter of kittens. Returning home, he breathlessly informed his mother that there were two boy kittens and two girl kittens.
> "How did you know?" his mother asked.
> "Daddy picked them up and looked underneath," he replied. "I think it's printed on the bottom."

At age five, my grandson, Aaron, provides me with an endless source of amusing stories. When he and I were coloring one afternoon, I asked him the name of the cartoon character on my page. He hesitated for a moment. "That's . . . No, wait . . ." He closed his eyes tightly, scrunched up his eyebrows, and tilted his head upward as if the answer might come from heaven. "It's Dot!" he suddenly shouted. "Yep, it's Dot. I just had to stop and listen to my brain for a minute."

3. *See your life as a sitcom.* Step back from your difficulties and look at them from the point of view of a TV director. Wouldn't some of your husband's foibles (and yours) make great scripts for comedies?

Many "husband" characters on TV can be insensitive and childish, but we rarely feel animosity toward them. In fact, we find them rather endearing. Why? Because it's usually clear that their wives love them. TV sitcom wives tend to respond with witty retorts rather than anger or bitterness, and life goes on.

In your real-life sitcom, you too can accomplish more with a light, good-natured tone than with a harsh, demanding one. When my husband tries to help with a task I'd prefer to tackle myself, I'm tempted to say, "Leave me alone!" Instead, I utter a phrase our grandson used when he was a toddler and had trouble pronouncing the letter *L*: "Yeave me ayone!" Ken gets the message, and we both have a good laugh.

Be careful, though, not to use humor at your husband's expense. When I was a youngster, during a dinner party for my mom's bridge group, I decided to make my debut in the world of practical jokes. My girlfriend Marilyn and I passed around a lovely box of candies. It wasn't until the ladies had popped the sweets into their mouths that we blurted out the truth: "They are chocolate-covered ants!"

Marilyn and I fell to the floor in a hysterical fit, but then realized we were the only ones laughing. Mom glared at me as her horrified friends hastily reached for their napkins and spit half-chewed ant carcasses into them.

The ladies' reaction stunned me. Where was their sense of humor? I never fully understood why our little joke bombed until I read these wise words of humorist Patsy Clairmont: "Humor: If it is at someone else's expense, it isn't funny."[1]

4. *Go on a humor hunt.* You may have to look hard for the humor in some of the things your spouse does, but it's worth the effort.

My mother, who is 90 years old as I write this, has been a good example of someone who can find humor in every situation. Her church maintains a tradition of asking members to stand and announce their birthdays, and to donate a dollar to missions for every year of their age. This practice was becoming costly for my mother. On her 84th birthday she stood up and, with a twinkle in her eye, declared, "I'm 84, and I ain't gonna pay no more!"

She continued to give, however, and on her 89th birthday was in church again. Her birthday proclamation was preceded by that of a five-year-old boy who held up five fingers and proudly announced, "I'm this many!"

Not to be outdone, my mom stood and held up five fingers. "I'm this many," she said, "plus 84 more."

My mom could refuse to admit her age, or grumble about indignities like sickness, frailty, and widowhood. Instead, she has looked for the humor in her situation. As one of her friends noted on a Christmas card, "For a bunch of old gals, we sure have a lot of fun." Those "old gals," most of whom are in their 70s and 80s, have been playing bridge for 40 years—the same bridge group that fell victim to my disastrous ant caper. It's a wonder they didn't disband that evening!

## Enter Laughing

When it comes to facing difficult situations—whether it's old age or having your husband around too much—it's all a matter of attitude. If you go into the situation depressed, feeling certain it's going to be a trial, it probably will be. As Isaac Singer put it, "If you keep saying that things are going to be bad, you have the chance of becoming a prophet." But if you go into your new situation with a sense of humor, determined to make the best of it, you'll find that "'tis to laugh."

It's been said that the most wasted of all days is the one on which you have not laughed.[2] I trust you haven't wasted today!

# 8

# Give Me a Break

☯

*Some people ask the secret of our long marriage.*
*We take time to go to a restaurant two times a week.*
*A little candlelight, dinner, music, and dancing.*
*She goes on Tuesday. I go Fridays.*
—HENNY YOUNGMAN

The biblical story of Ruth and Naomi is a charming tale of loyalty. It features Ruth's beautiful pledge, "Where you go I will go, and where you stay I will stay. Your people will be my people and your God my God" (Ruth 1:16).

While I applaud Ruth's total commitment to her mother-in-law, I can't help but wonder what she would do with a retired or work-at-home husband. Would she be so adamant about sticking close to him at all times, or would she jump on the nearest donkey and head for the hills?

Everybody needs an occasional escape hatch. Even the best of marriages can suffer from too much togetherness. Take my friend Barbara (name changed), for example. I often ran into her at the library or mall. Since I knew her husband had taken an early retirement, I would always ask, "How's it going with Rick?"

"Fine" was her usual reply. "And how are things with you and Ken?" I would then render a long tale of woe, usually injected with plenty of humor. But Barbara never nodded as if she understood. She just shook her head in dismay, or opened her large, blue eyes wide in apparent disbelief.

Her reaction seemed understandable; I knew her husband, a pleasant, easy-going guy with a great sense of humor. Surely he would never be in the way or make demands on her time.

Barbara and Rick seemed to have weathered the spouse-in-the-house storm so successfully that I thought they'd be the perfect couple to interview for this book. When I approached Barbara about offering hope to other women by sharing her story, her eyes widened. "What do you mean?" she gasped. "Rick is driving me crazy! Why do you think you keep running into me at the mall and the library all the time?"

Finally she opened up, telling me the surprising story of a once fun-loving guy who now spent his days on the couch with a bag of Doritos in his lap, a can of soda in one hand and a remote control welded to the other. The constant drone of the TV had driven Barbara to seek escape at the library and mall. Returning from her outings, she would be greeted by a husband pleading that she dish up a meal ASAP. Evidently those Doritos weren't all that filling.

It was clear to me then that, as the saying goes, "The grass is not always greener on the other side of the fence." And as another wise person added, "Even if it is, it still has to be mowed."

## The Great Escapes

There's no need to feel guilty when you find yourself think-ing, "I've got to get out of here!" Chances are your husband has the same thoughts at times, and will not only understand your need to get away, but will also enjoy having the house to himself for a while. When you return in a better frame of mind, he probably will be relieved and grateful.

Here are some tips for short, sweet getaways:

1. *Be prepared.* Have a few escape spots in mind, so that when pressures build and you're overcome with the desire to flee, you'll know which direction to head. In addition to the library and mall, one of my favorite escape hatches is a nearby park, where I enjoy a brisk walk or sitting on a bench and watching the children play. Now that none of the kids screaming, "Mommy, look at me!" are mine, it's a relaxing pastime.

2. *Get energized.* An afternoon at the movie theater can crank up your imagination. Some women prefer escaping to the gym, where exercise gets those endorphins flowing; after a brisk workout, they feel more able to cope. Having lunch with a friend is another good way to vent frustration and gain strength to meet challenges. I highly recommend this escape, as staff members at my favorite restaurant can verify. Their corner booth has an imprint of my derriere permanently embedded in it, and they are considering installing a plaque with my name on the wall beside it.

3. *Soak away stress.* You don't always have to leave home to escape. A relaxing bubble bath can do wonders for your disposition. While you're soaking, surround yourself with scented candles. Soothing music can also relax you and put you in a better mood. Pop a praise CD or tape into your stereo

system and reflect on the inspiring words. Or choose classics like Mozart to take you away from it all.

4. *Find time to read.* A good book can provide escape anywhere. In my workshops I frequently quote from one of my favorite "feel good" books, Barbara Johnson's *Living Somewhere Between Estrogen and Death.* When I do, the ladies invariably ask, "But how do you find time to read?" The question always surprises me. From the time I first learned to recite "See Dick run," I've been in love with the written word. So I make reading a priority. I give myself permission to read—even in the middle of the day, even if the dishes aren't done and dinner isn't prepared. Sadly, many women tell me the only time they feel justified reading is when they're waiting for a doctor's appointment. Give yourself permission to enjoy a book!

5. *Rediscover childhood.* When was the last time you sprawled on the floor with a box of crayons and a coloring book in front of you? As a grandmother who frequently engages in this activity, I can assure you it's still as relaxing and satisfying as when we were youngsters. (Getting up from the sprawled position, however, is a bit more difficult at this age.) Blowing bubbles is another childlike activity that's fun for adults. Grab an inexpensive bottle of the soapy stuff, dip your wand in, and blow softly. Then enjoy the glorious sight of glistening bubbles floating over the treetops. If it's been an especially stressful day, imagine yourself on board one of the bubbles!

6. *Take up a hobby.* Scrapbooking is one relaxing pastime worth trying. My friend Wendy introduced me to this delightful hobby of chronicling family history in photos and artwork. I dragged out our boxes of family photos, made copies of the older, more fragile images of my ancestors, and am preserving them in albums for my children and grandchild. Look for classes offered through craft stores, community centers, or

a senior center. Or purchase supplies and instructional books and do your own thing!

## Separate Vacations?

So far I've described nearby escapes that involve only a few hours away from your husband. Now I'd like to suggest some serious time out.

How about separate vacations?

After you pick yourself up from the floor, hear me out. If your and your husband's ideas of "vacation" differ drastically, and if you're willing to allow each other a week apart, then why not take separate vacations from time to time? I've been there, done that, and am a better person because of it.

Ken and I don't define "vacation" in the same way. I'm drawn to the ocean; it soothes my nerves and feeds my soul. Ken, on the other hand, sunburns easily and hates the gritty feeling of sand between his toes. His idea of a vacation is to cover ground; to him, the journey *is* the vacation. I prefer to go to one lovely spot and stay put.

So at this time in our lives, we're learning to compromise. Now that our children are grown, the days of separate vacations have begun.

For the last few summers I've spent one week at an ocean resort not far from our home. For a few evenings during that week, Ken meets me at the harbor for a fish and chips dinner followed by a breathtaking sunset. He willingly lets me have this time at the beach, probably because he's so grateful that he doesn't have to be there all day. I suspect that he also enjoys having the house to himself.

That week is a wonderful time of renewal for me. When it's over, I return to my husband—restored, replenished, and a whole lot nicer to be around.

As for Ken, family business matters require him to make yearly trips to Texas. Occasionally I accompany him, but he often prefers to make the journey by himself. He is free to drive to his heart's content, and can reach his destination a day earlier than he would if I were in the car. We've both come to appreciate this arrangement (as you may recall, that week is my chance to purge leftovers from the refrigerator).

And we still take *some* trips together.

## Serendipity Moments

Most escapes may be planned, but it's good to stay open to unexpected opportunities for escape. My friend Carolynn refers to these as "serendipity moments." I had one such moment recently when, during a particularly stressful morning, my grandson, Aaron, and his mom appeared on my doorstep. I'd completely forgotten that it was my day to watch him, and I had several errands that couldn't be put off. Knowing how bored Aaron would be, I decided to combine my necessary trip to San Diego with a drive along the coast. When I told him of these plans, he had a better idea.

"Nana, do we have to just drive by the ocean? Can't we stop and play in it?"

My first thought was that this would involve packing a lunch and loading up the car with the ice chest, beach chairs, umbrellas, sand shovels, and buckets. Having neither the time nor the energy to make such preparations, however, I decided to grab a serendipity moment. Tossing beach towels, a bottle of water, and a bag of cheese crackers into the car, Aaron and I were off for a marvelous adventure. At the beach, Aaron amused himself by digging a hole in the sand and watching it fill with water. Watching him dance about joyfully, I let the sound of the waves and the cool ocean breeze take me away from it all.

If you don't have an ocean or a grandson at your disposal, you can still enjoy some serendipity moments. Why not grab some cheese and crackers for an impromptu picnic in your own backyard?

If you can't physically get away, why not pick up the phone and call that friend you've been thinking about? Or invite your neighbor over for a cup of tea. A serendipity moment is anything you do just for fun, spontaneously.

No matter which of these escapes you choose, enjoy yourself. You *do* deserve a break today—and tomorrow, as well!

# 9

# No More Couch Potatoes

꩜

*Years ago we discovered the exact point, the dead center of middle age. It occurs when you are too young to take up golf and too old to rush up to the net.*
—FRANKLIN PIERCE ADAMS

Inactivity usually isn't a problem for husbands who've come home to work. But for those who are retired, it can be a disease that affects both spouses.

Ever notice that the word "retired" ends in "tired?" Maybe that's because people go into retirement too tired to do anything but sit in front of the TV all day. Or perhaps they get so busy with activities that they tire quickly. I hope you choose the second option, because couch potatoes are mostly a dull lot.

The at-home years are the time for you and your husband

to tackle all those things you dreamed of doing but never did. I hope your dreams are big ones. Remember that saying: "It's never too late to be what you might have been."

## Don't Stop Now

A former college classmate had always appeared shy. She confided to me, however, that she'd always wanted to be an actress but hadn't had the nerve to try. Now, in middle age, she thought, "What is the worst thing that can happen? So they turn me down. I'm a big girl now, I can take it." She joined a local community theater group and landed a leading part! I'd like to think she's bound for the Great White Way.

Do you have a secret desire to act, dance, play the piano, or climb a mountain? Dr. Sherwood "Woody" Wirt climbed Mt. Fuji at the age of 72; at this writing, he dreams of climbing even more mountains. Why stop now? He's only 90!

Woody and his wife, Ruth, have mastered the art of growing old together gracefully, and embody the keys to a successful retirement. They maintain a strong faith and a good sense of humor. They also keep busy with separate and shared activities.

Though officially retired from his job as editor of *Decision* magazine, Woody has continued to write—28 books at last count. An ordained minister, he fills the pulpit as guest pastor for numerous churches and mentors members of his San Diego Christian Writers' Guild.

Ruth leads a women's Bible study and helps with senior ministry in their church. When she isn't accompanying Woody on his book tours, she likes to knit and sew. Despite being busy with their own activities, Ruth and Woody find time for golfing and hiking—the two events that top their list of fun things to do together.

When I asked Ruth for her thoughts on Woody's retirement, she replied, "What retirement?" The Wirts had just returned from a cross-country book tour and were preparing to leave again to visit family before embarking on another whirlwind trip.

This couple's life has been exciting and full of hope—and yours can be too, if you and your spouse find activities to enjoy together.

## Sticks in the Mud and Internet Spuds

Perhaps you already know what *you* want to do. But you may have trouble getting your mate interested in anything besides the sports channels. Some husbands are "sticks in the mud." They're quick to point out that this is *their* retirement, so would we please just leave them alone and let them do as they please?

We wives might be happy to honor this request if our husbands' plans didn't involve us. Sometimes the husband who wants to lie around the house all day wants his wife by his side the whole time. Even if he doesn't mind her doing "her thing," his camping out in the living room makes it difficult for her to invite friends in and usually requires a litter patrol by the end of the day.

Every husband deserves rest and relaxation. But an inert state can lead to depression—his *and* yours! For his own sake, he needs to pursue a few activities, if for no other reason than to keep those little gray cells working.

TV-addicted couch potatoes aren't the only ones on the "inactive" list. There are plenty of Internet spuds, too. These junkies spend their time surfing the Web, visiting chat rooms, or ordering all those "amazing finds" that can be delivered to your doorstep in 24 hours or less. While the Internet can be a fantastic research tool, it can become a dangerous addiction for many people. Encourage your husband to limit his time on the Internet, and to spend more time at activities that are healthier for both mind and body. If you suspect your husband might be struggling with an Internet addiction like pornography or gambling, see your pastor for help—or contact an organization like Focus on the Family (see "Where to Get Help" in the Appendix of this book).

## Centering with Seniors

If your husband has never been a joiner, you might want to steer him to the nearest senior center. This may be easier said than done, of course. When one wife attempted this with her 75-year-old husband, he grunted and shook his head.

"Why not?" she asked.

"Too many old people there," he muttered.

Still, it's worth a try. Explain to your husband that, in this case, "joining" is simply a matter of joining in the fun. You may wish to get involved too.

While individual centers differ in what they offer, many include everything from old favorites like shuffleboard to new ones like computer training. You might find craft rooms, libraries, and lecture halls, as well as courses in writing memoirs, tracing roots, folk dancing, photography, and woodworking. Need more physical activity? Look for low-impact exercise classes.

## His and Hers Activities

When choosing things to do, remember to do some separately. These involvements give you new topics of conversation to bring back to each other, and allow you to make different acquaintances. Remember the early days of your marriage, when both of you probably led busy lives and were happy to be together at the end of the day? With some separate interests, at the end of the day you'll be especially glad to see each other again.

Some of the activities couples choose to share include classes through community colleges or recreation departments, square dancing, gardening, community theater, traveling, hiking, kayaking, and fishing. I've heard of one brave lady who fishes side by side with her husband on an inner tube! If poor health or tight finances prevent you from doing such things, or if you simply prefer a quiet evening at home, try working on a jigsaw puzzle or a game of Scrabble.

Some women complain that their husbands are loners who want only to do things with their wives. As flattering as this might sound, the wives are less than thrilled with the situation. Nor do counselors see it as a sign of a healthy marriage. "You should never expect your spouse to be everything to you," pastor Terrence Sherry advises. "That puts unfair expectations on your partner. Men need to spend time with their men friends and women need time with their women friends."

Many couples concur. As one husband told me, "If my wife were everything to me, then I would be into sewing and knitting." He believes men need to be with their male friends in order to maintain their masculinity. And in her book *Keys to Living with a Retired Husband*, Gloria Bledsoe Goodman points out, "Compatibility is not so much doing things together as it's feeling safe to do things separately."[1]

Spend time with other couples. Invite them for dinner and a rousing game of Trivial Pursuit or Pictionary. You'll sharpen your minds and enjoy the companionship.

What if, in spite of your best efforts, your mate insists that he doesn't want to engage in activities with others? Try to get him interested in a hobby and encourage him to pursue it with passion. On his next birthday, Christmas, or Father's Day, subscribe to a magazine related to his interests, or purchase some supplies for his hobby. Do what it takes to pull your husband out of his "I don't want to do anything, and you are all I need" mood.

## Nothing in Common?

Some wives complain of the opposite problem. Their spouses have plenty of plans, but none of them appeal to the wives. A friend of mine dreads her husband's retirement because he plans to do nothing but travel.

As a homebody, she doesn't look forward to traipsing around the country and feeling rootless. She and her spouse have some serious compromising sessions ahead of them. Perhaps he'll agree to fewer trips, while she might look on their travels as an opportunity to discover subjects for the painting and photography she enjoys.

Another woman, whose husband also has traveling and photography on his mind, is already planning her adjustment strategy. She's stocking up on books to read while her husband takes pictures for the book he plans to publish. "I will be content to sit in the motor home and read while he does his thing," she insists. Married for 42 years, they have been partners in a studio photography business for over 27 years. After working together for so long, they feel certain they can survive the retirement years with all of its togetherness. With their positive attitude, I'm sure they will.

## Lending a Hand

If your husband is retired, did he envision spending his "golden" years on the golf links? I hope he's not as addicted to the game as the bridegroom who brought his clubs to his wedding ceremony. Confronted by his bride, he asked, "Well, this isn't going to take all day, is it?"

If this sounds like your spouse, he may be shocked to discover that a person can only golf or fish for so long before a sense of discontentment sets in. That's when you should point out the rewards of living for more than just oneself. Introduce him to the wonderful world of volunteer work.

Perhaps you're already familiar with this world. Maybe you've helped out with Cub Scouts, Girl Scouts, your child's classroom, or Sunday school. If so, you know the rewards of service to others—that warm feeling that comes from being needed, and the joy of making a difference in someone's life.

Volunteering can be a great way to learn humility, too. I learned this on my first visit to a nursing home, determined to lead a well-researched study on the Book of Galatians. Passing out large-print copies of the first chapter, I watched as one man carefully folded his papers into fourths, placed them in his shirt pocket, and buttoned the pocket with a smug smile of accomplishment. Nearby, a lady in a wheelchair let her chapter slide to the floor as she nodded off to sleep; several other residents quickly followed suit.

One woman, though, seemed especially alert. She kept her eyes on me and continually nodded as if in agreement. *Wow, I've really got her hooked,* I thought. After reading a few verses, I asked, "What do you think Paul is trying to tell us here?"

The lady looked me straight in the eye. With a firm, loud voice she replied, "The blue whale jumped over the moon."

So much for my greatness as a Bible study leader.

Whether or not you need such a humbling experience, you probably realize that Jesus calls us to be servants. By following His command, you do what my pastor, Dr. Bruce Humphrey, encourages all of us to do: Make Jesus smile!

Now it's time for Jesus to smile on your husband. Help your mate discover how to use his talents to benefit others.

## Where Do I Start?

During the career years, men are often too busy with their jobs to sign up for outside responsibilities. When retirement hits, they may not know how to volunteer. Steer your husband to the "volunteers needed" section of your local paper, or open his eyes to the pleas for help printed in your church newsletter. He'll soon learn that when it comes to volunteering, there is no shortage of jobs available—and no need to worry about downsizing or mandatory retirement age.

Your own church is the best place to get started. In addition to ushering, music or drama or youth ministry, Sunday school classes, running the sound system, visitation, and stacking chairs, he may find outreach programs that minister to your community.

Since our area is home to a large retirement population, our church has found a way to take advantage of the wisdom and skills of its older members. Our Helping Hands program offers seniors assistance with home-maintenance chores. The volunteers say no job is too big or too small; they'll change a lightbulb or build a wheelchair ramp. This work is ideal for men who like to tinker. If your church doesn't have a similar program, you might want to talk to your husband about starting one.

## What to Do?

When choosing volunteer work, your husband may pick an area based on skills from the workplace. Or he could go in another direction, perhaps pursuing an interest for which he's never had time.

Either way, there's no shortage of opportunities. A husband who enjoys woodworking, for example, might teach this skill to youngsters through the Boys and Girls Club or YMCA. Or he might build sets for a local theater group, or create toys to donate for a charitable auction. If he loves sports, he could volunteer to coach a youth league. Then there are opportunities like Meals on Wheels, programs for helping kids learn to swim, police department senior volunteer patrols, literacy programs, hospital auxiliaries, visiting veterans' hospitals, guiding museum tours, helping hospice patients, working with prison ministries, and sharing business expertise with entrepreneurs and nonprofit organizations. The possibilities are endless.

Despite the humbling experience I've already mentioned, my favorite place to volunteer is nursing homes. They've proven to me that the Lord has a great sense of humor. Why else would He call me to conduct a hymn sing at a nursing home when I can't carry a tune in a bucket? I was initially drawn to this ministry in an attempt to pay back the thoughtful women who helped my dad when he lived in a nursing home out-of-state. Every week they wheeled him into the dining room for hymn singing and a short sermon. The week before his death, Mom found him sitting up in bed, singing, "Jesus Loves Me."

Shortly after Dad's passing, a friend asked if I could take over her nursing home ministry. I agreed—before realizing that the job required musical talent! I soon discovered, however, that the residents realized I was singing from my heart (it was obvious that I wasn't singing from my diaphragm). They didn't care what I sounded like. They just liked having me visit them each week. No doubt their tolerance was also due to the fact that their hearing wasn't quite what it once was—a real blessing in this case.

Nursing homes are one of the few places where Christians are welcome to share their faith. Through room visitations, decorating bulletin boards, reading to residents, helping them write letters, or leading a more structured activity such as a hymn sing or arts and crafts class, you can serve others and share God's love with them. After 15 years in this ministry, I'm still inspired by the dear men and women who have learned the art of being content in whatever circumstances God has placed them. And I've learned that when you help others, you reap much more than you sow.

## Get Unretired!

Sometimes volunteer work can turn into a part-time job. Some men, restless with too much leisure, find this very satisfying. My neighbor Gus is a good example. Though he busied himself with a square dancing club, woodworking, and American Legion activities, he was overjoyed when fellow Legion members offered him the adjutant position (in non-military terms, that's "secretary"). He picks up the Legion's mail, handles correspondence, and arranges special events. Recently I caught him dashing out the door on his way to a conference in Palm Springs. I don't know whose grin was bigger—his or his wife's!

In a national survey conducted by Peter D. Hart Associates, only 28 percent of Americans in the 50-75 age group saw retirement in the traditional way—as a time of leisure and recreation. A full 65 percent preferred to stay active and contribute to society. More people than ever are looking for opportunities that offer meaning and a chance to make a difference in the world.[2]

In an article entitled, "The New Unretirement," Marc Freedman concludes that ". . . if in their earlier years, work fed the body, men and women in their later years are now looking for ways to better serve the soul."[3] Perhaps your soul, and your husband's, need serving too.

# PART III

# Cherishing Your Situation

✪

*Marriage is our last, best chance to grow up.*
—Joseph Barth

# 10

# To Husbands with Love

☯

*A successful marriage requires falling in love many times, always with the same person.*
—MIGNON MCLAUGHLIN

When I asked retired husbands what they needed from their wives, they replied with these answers:

- Affection
- Acceptance
- Kindness
- Patience
- Support
- Understanding

Wouldn't your husband—retired or not—like to receive the love gifts on this wish list? Let's look at some ways to make his wishes come true, starting with affection, acceptance, and kindness. We'll consider the rest in the next chapter.

## Affectionately Yours

Expressing affection is an essential element in meeting your husband's needs. But it's not enough to simply say, "I love you." Men believe actions speak louder than words—that "nothin' says lovin'" like washing the dishes, taking out the trash, gassing up the car, or agreeing to a long visit from a mother-in-law. To your husband, these acts are the equivalent of a dozen roses and a box of chocolates. Each is a whispered "I love you," but without all the romance!

Some husbands tend to doubt the value of "mushy" displays of affection. Ken, being the practical man that he is, once questioned my desire for flowers. "They are just going to die," he explained. It only took a second for him to realize that *he* might be the one close to expiring if he continued to use that type of logic.

Most men just can't help looking at the practical side of things. So when trying to convey affection to your spouse, be sure to include plenty of down-to-earth expressions. One of the best ways you can whisper "I love you" to your husband is to make time for him.

Yes, you need plenty of activities for yourself. But avoid getting so busy that you neglect your spouse. If he enjoys traveling, your schedule should be flexible enough to allow for an occasional day trip—or more—together. It's fine to maintain your membership in favorite organizations, but the at-home adjustment period may not be the best time to take on the office of president or committee chairman.

Expressions of affection don't need to be elaborate or showy. The most genuine often spring from simple, daily activities. For example, why not express your love by preparing your husband's favorite food? A special meal is a surefire way to make your mate feel appreciated.

And don't overlook simple gestures such as hugs, kisses, and hand-holding—tried and true ways of expressing affection. We're never too old for these acts of fondness. Slip your hand into his whether you're strolling on a moonlit beach or walking through the mall's parking lot. For some couples those gestures may include tactfully helping a husband over a curb or giving him a back rub with BenGay. Not exactly romantic moves—but they definitely say, "I care for you."

## Acceptance: A Place to Be Himself

"I like you just the way you are," Mr. Rogers always assured his young viewers. You need to relay this same message of acceptance to your husband.

This is especially true at retirement. Your mate needs reassurance that he is valued apart from his career. The identities of many men are so intertwined with their work that when they retire, they feel worthless. As one pointed out, "The first thing men ask when they get together is, 'How's the job going?' "

Remind your husband of all the things about him that you love. Make it clear that your view of him hasn't changed just because his job situation has; he's the same person now that he was before he retired.

Whether your husband has come home to retire or to work, he needs another kind of acceptance, too—the assurance that you're glad to have him around the house. (If you've been applying some of the tips from the "Bettering Your Situation" section, you should be able to say this and mean it.)

All too often, at-home men feel like intruders. "I don't feel comfortable in my own home" is a complaint I often hear. This is especially true of men whose dwellings are decorated in a formal style. Having been chastised for sitting on a valuable antique, these poor men don't know where to take the load off their feet. Nor do they know where to step. Highly polished wood floors and light-colored carpets scream, "Keep Off!" Even the milder admonition, "Make sure your shoes are clean," is not husband-friendly.

It took an embarrassing moment for me to finally lighten up about the cleanliness of my home. Preparing to host a Bible study luncheon, I ignored our leader's plea to "not go to any trouble." Racing around in a cleaning frenzy, I drove my family crazy. I was still scrubbing minutes before the first guest arrived. After the luncheon went off without a hitch, I was feeling pretty proud of myself as I ushered the last guest through my sparkling-clean front door. It was then that I saw it: Lying smack dab in the middle of my well-polished hall table was the toilet bowl brush, accompanied by the economy-sized bottle of toilet bowl cleanser!

Here are some tips for making your husband feel more at home:

1. Take a look around your residence. Is it furnished with pieces that are meant for viewing rather than sitting? If so, consider replacing at least one item with a comfortable easy chair for your husband.

2. Try not to be obsessed with cleanliness. If you've raised children, you probably remember childproofing your home. You stashed away those breakable collectibles. You selected easy-to-clean fabrics and a carpet that would hide stains. If something broke or got dirty, you tried not to lash out at the perpetrator. Your spouse deserves the same consideration. Husbands tell me they would appreciate the right to "chill out," put their feet up on the coffee table, and snack to their

heart's content. And they want to do this without a "look" from their wives.

3. Lighten up about keeping the house in order. Women often complain that they're constantly having to pick up after their at-home husbands. If this is a problem for you, suggest to your spouse that he tidy up after himself. Or you could opt for another popular strategy: confining the mess to one room. Most husbands will respect a wife's request to keep the living room presentable if they're allowed leeway in another room.

4. Help your husband find his own space. Perhaps the ideal solution is to establish a wife-free zone. If your house doesn't have a den, consider converting a spare bedroom into one. You might have to make a weekly run to retrieve dirty plates and cups, but respect the room as his inner sanctum and steer clear (for your sanity as well as his). If your abode is too small for this, designate areas in one room that each of you can call your own. In that way, at least the mess will be confined to one spot.

Of course, it's not always the husband who's the messy one. My disorderly traits frustrate Ken, who lives by the old military rule, "A place for everything and everything in its place." Imagine his chagrin when I purchased a plaque that read, "Dull Women Have Immaculate Houses."

"You are actually going to advertise the fact that you are a sloppy housekeeper?" he asked as I nailed the colorful plaque to our family room wall.

"No, I'm advertising my philosophy, that's all," I explained.

Whatever your housekeeping philosophy, try not to insist on perfection. When your husband comes home to roost, allow *him* to be less than perfect too. That's the best way to demonstrate your acceptance.

## How Kind of You!

Over the past 15 years, I've observed many activity directors in the nursing home where I minister every week. Some are extremely efficient; others forget I'm coming. Some are more than glad to make copies of songs; others grumble under their breath. Their mood doesn't matter to me; I gladly come each week no matter what the reception.

But their mood does make a difference to the residents. Since many of these elderly men and women are without family or friends, staff members are their only source of companionship. I've seen forlorn patients, slumped in their wheelchairs, suddenly straighten up and smile when a friendly activity director gives them a gentle pat on the back. Nurse's aides who give hugs freely are as priceless as diamonds. These workers may be efficient, organized, knowledgeable, and innovative—but if they lack *kindness*, their skills matter not to the residents.

As wives, we can be intelligent, organized, efficient, and even charming—but if we don't offer our husbands kindness, how effective are we?

The apostle Paul put it this way: "If I speak in the tongues of men and of angels, but have not love, I am only a resounding gong or a clanging cymbal. If I have the gift of prophecy and can fathom all mysteries and all knowledge, and if I have a faith that can move mountains, but have not love, I am nothing.... Love is patient, love is kind" (1 Corinthians 13:1-2,4).

What does kindness look like in a marriage? One 10 year-old boy defined it as "telling your wife she's beautiful, even if she looks like a truck."

Here's *my* list:

- Kindness is saying, "Go for it!" even when you think your husband's dream is impractical.
- Kindness is agreeing to see an action/adventure movie when you would rather watch a romantic comedy.
- Kindness is welcoming his buddies into your home—even the "weird guy."
- Kindness is forgetting the one anniversary when *he* forgot.
- Kindness is saying, "Enjoy your fishing trip!" when the lawn needs mowing.

Kindness is love. And remember—love is patient.

# 11

# Relishing Retirement

## ல/ல

*Retirement is when you stop living at work,
and begin working at living.*
—AUTHOR UNKNOWN

By now you've gleaned some hints for dealing with—and even appreciating—your around-the-house husband. Whether he's working from a home office or retired, you know how to handle all that togetherness.

But retirement poses special challenges—for you and your spouse. How can the two of you cherish that situation?

That's what this chapter is about. Read it if your mate is retired—or if you think he might be someday.

## The Wonder Years?

As you face retirement, you and your husband need each other more than ever. You need each other for physical support as you battle arthritic hips and deteriorating kneecaps.

You need each other for emotional support as you face life's changes.

This support is especially vital if your "golden years" aren't quite as glorious as you'd hoped. You may have elderly parents who need your care, or adult children who've come home to roost after making poor choices. Maybe you're the primary caregiver for grandchildren. Perhaps poor health keeps you from activities you love.

But even if retirement is everything the two of you hoped for, your spouse still needs your support. Retirement, like any other transition, is stressful.

Try to remember a life transition *you've* weathered. Perhaps it was when you left for college, got married, or had a child. Didn't you need support to get through those difficult days?

I certainly needed my husband's support when he carted me off to Texas to meet his relatives for the first time. I felt a bit like a prize heifer being rounded up to parade in front of the judges at the local fair. When I was stricken with stomach flu en route, I figured I was in big trouble. After all, a diseased cow is pretty much worthless.

Ken booked a motel room for us, then phoned his Aunt Mabel to let her know that the dinner party—which was to include a huge passel of kinfolk—would have to be postponed. He declined Aunt Mabel's advice that he purchase a bucket from the hardware store, toss me and it in the backseat, and drive on.

Next day (after a stop at the hardware store) we arrived at the farmhouse. No one in the dining room seemed to notice the greenish tinge in my complexion as an endless stream of "taters" and other "fixins" were passed under my nose. My refusal to sample anything was not well received; worse, our one-day delay had caused Aunt Mabel's prized strawberry pie to "turn all runny." There would be no blue ribbon for *this* heifer.

Fortunately, Ken smoothed things over—making it possible for us to enjoy many more dinners on the farm. His relatives turned out to be mighty fine folks—and mighty fine chefs, too.

So support your husband during his retirement transition. Keep in mind, though, that as Philip R. Alper, M.D. writes, "Even in the best of circumstances, the transitions involved in retirement do create the potential for depression. The trick is to navigate past the dangers and focus on the many opportunities. Keeping mentally and physically active, thinking positively, and staying busy are still the best strategies."[1]

We wives are good at navigating. So let's pitch in and help our husbands through the murky waters ahead. First, let's look at some ways to ease their concerns.

## Concerns and Compassion

Just what *are* your husband's concerns about retirement, anyway? You can't meet his needs if you don't know what they are. And you can't know what they are if he doesn't tell you, right?

Well, if that's true, we're all in a lot of trouble. Most men are reluctant to discuss their feelings. And they certainly don't want to be caught looking needy. So it's up to you to surmise your husband's needs.

One of the easiest ways to do this is to put yourself in his shoes. Imagine someone telling you that your job, either as a housewife or a worker outside the home, is over: "You are no longer needed. Thank you for your time. Hand over your apron (or clean out your desk and say good-bye to your co-workers). Go find something else to do with the rest of your life. Oh, I almost forgot. I know that time doesn't matter any more, but here's a gold watch."

Now imagine that, on top of this humiliating scenario, your mate isn't too happy to have you around. He thinks you're invading his territory.

How do you feel? Frightened, lonely, rejected? Your husband may feel that way too.

To help him, what do you need? Compassion!

One dictionary defines compassion as "sympathetic consciousness of another's distress together with a desire to alleviate." Included in the long list of synonyms for "compassionate" are these noble traits—gracious, indulgent, pardoning, benevolent, tender, merciful, pitying, lenient, mild, indulgent, and forgiving.

Whew! On a good day, you might manage about a tenth of the attitudes listed. It would seem that if you're to be compassionate (assuming that the word "Saint" does not precede your first name), you face quite a challenge.

When you look at Gloria Goodman's definition of compassion, however, it doesn't seem as difficult. According to her, "Compassion is the essence of love."[2]

Love is something you can handle. But it's not enough to *feel* love for your husband; you need to *act* on those feelings. "Dear children, let us not love with words or tongue but with actions and in truth" (1 John 3:18).

Here are several actions you can take.

## Action 1: Be Patient

Abraham Lincoln said, "The best thing about the future is that it comes only one day at a time." So we might as well be patient about it.

Patience plays an important role during the early stages of

your husband's retirement. He needs time to relax and adjust; resist the temptation to nag him about all the tasks you were saving for when he retired.

After a reasonable period of idleness, however, gently encourage him to start establishing a routine. At first, empty days with nothing planned sound good to a man whose hours have always been structured. But in time the emptiness can become frightening.

## Action 2: Plan Together

If your husband isn't convinced that retirement planning is a must, remind him of this sage advice from baseball legend Yogi Berra:

"You've got to be very careful if you don't know where you're going because you might not get there." If that's not enough, toss in one more sports reference from an unknown wise person: "In life, as in football, you won't go far unless you know where the goalposts are."

Fortunately, planning can be fun. As you and your husband discuss your hopes and dreams, try asking basic questions of each other about your retirement priorities and desires. Here are some from the authors of *Growing Older Together*.[3]

- Do I like where I'm living now and hope to stay here?
- What changes would make me happier? Do I want to move? If so, where? Far away? Nearby?
- What do I like doing now and want to continue?
- What do I hate doing and would like to give up?
- What bores me? What excites me?
- What do I like doing with my spouse?
- What do I like doing alone?
- What gives me the greatest satisfaction?

The authors of these questions caution that your answers must be honest—and realistic. "There's no point in dreaming of living in the White House or becoming a tightrope walker,"[4] they note. If your and your spouse's answers clash, ask yourself what kinds of compromises can be worked out.

## Action 3: Take Your Time

While it's important to discuss your dreams, avoid acting on them too quickly. Stability is important for both of you as you adjust to your new lifestyle, and psychologists warn that life-changing decisions shouldn't be made in times of stress.

For example, don't rush to get in on the following "once in a lifetime" opportunities you might see advertised:

- MAKE $$$ GETTING PEOPLE TO PUT SIGNS LIKE THIS ON TELEPHONE POLES!
- AVAILABLE NOW: BEAUTIFUL CONDO IN DOWNTOWN DES MOINES. WITHIN WALKING DISTANCE OF THE BEACH.
- FOR SALE CHEAP: TWENTY ACRES OF PRIME FLORIDA SWAMPLAND. ALLIGATORS INCLUDED.

In other words, don't jump into something you may be sorry for later. Don't take up a vagabond life without giving such matters a great deal of thought. If you believe you want to travel, experiment with some trial excursions.

Think twice before selling your house, too. Eventually, weariness or ill health could force you to head for home. Sometimes couples hastily move to a new location and later regret it. If you're considering a move to a different part of the country, try renting in the area for a while to see if you want to permanently reside there.

If you're tempted to rush into a decision, try redirecting that energy into researching your options together. Make it an enjoyable project. Talk to others who are retired; check out books, magazine articles, organizations, lectures, and continuing education classes devoted to retirement issues. Don't forget the biggest research tool of all, the Internet. Examine the "Where to Get Help" section at the end of this book. And, of course, ask God for wisdom in your decision making.

## Action 4: Be Positive

Encourage your husband by concentrating on the positive aspects of your new lifestyle. No more alarm clocks, long commutes, or—if his job required it—suits and ties. (I have to agree with Linda Ellerbee, who said, "If men can rule the world, why can't they stop wearing neckties? How intelligent is it to start your day by tying a little noose around your neck?")

Remind your spouse of some more "upsides" of retirement as well.

Note that you now have time to focus on each other, and to pursue the things that interest you. Each positive remark you make about your situation and the new world ahead can reinforce your husband's wobbly emotional structure and prop him up when he's wavering internally.

L. James and Jackie Harvey, authors of *Every Day Is Saturday,* asked seniors, "What is the best thing about retirement?" Here are some answers they received:[5]

- I have less stress due to a schedule or my choice.
- We are able to share time together as husband and wife.
- Being able to read the newspaper thoroughly every day.
- I can go places when there's no traffic.
- You can now get involved with the community by volunteering in various activities.

• Watching my neighbors scrape the snow off their cars.

Help your spouse to see retirement as an adventure—not just a physical one, but an opportunity to learn new things and to think with a new attitude. A positive outlook will not only improve your husband's disposition—it can help keep him healthy as well, preventing the stress, anxiety, depression, and anger that can increase the risk of a heart attack.

## Action 5: Seek Spiritual Strength

The authors of *Every Day Is Saturday* observe, "Without faith in Christ Jesus, the 'golden years' will have no glitter at all. Without faith, the 'golden years' will be, at best, 'fool's gold.'[6]

They go on to remind us, "One of the best things about retirement is that we can enjoy faith more fully and continue to grow in that faith. An ever-maturing faith holds the key to joy in retirement and to preparation for the fantastic life to come when . . . we are transferred to the 'home office.' "[7]

As your husband turns to you for support during this transition, make sure the two of you remain strong in the Lord. Help your spouse develop his own "quiet time," and find time for devotions as a couple. Check your local bookstore or church library for books like *Moments Together for Couples* by Dennis and Barbara Rainey, and *Night Light* by Dr. James and Shirley Dobson—two of my favorites.

If you aren't already keeping a prayer journal, give it a try. You and your mate will be inspired and encouraged as you look back on God's faithfulness in your lives.

Does your spouse need to be reminded of the power of prayer? Tell him the following story, related by a pastor who insists it really happened:

It seems a kitten had climbed a tree in the pastor's backyard, but couldn't be coaxed down. The tree was too slender to climb, so the pastor tied a rope from the tree to his car and drove a few feet so that the tree bent down. Before he could reach up and get the kitten, the tree went *boing*—and the kitten sailed through the air, out of sight.

A few days later, a woman from his church told him that her little girl had been begging for a cat. The mom didn't want one, but finally told her daughter, "If God gives you a cat, I'll let you keep it." Then, as she told the pastor, "I watched my child go out in the yard, get on her knees, and ask God for a cat. And really, Pastor, you won't believe this, but I saw it with my own eyes. A kitten suddenly came flying out of the blue sky, with its paws outspread, and landed right in front of her."[8]

If that story isn't true, it should be.

Does your husband have trouble getting enthused about spiritual disciplines? Try talking about spiritual fitness—and how it parallels physical exercise. I've found a lot of similarities between my daily neighborhood walk and my walk with the Lord. You might want to share with your husband the following concepts I've learned:

1. *Start early.* Just as walking in the morning is exhilarating, meeting the Lord at the beginning of the day uplifts my soul. When I'm tempted to stay in bed a little longer, I remember that the Lord awaits and I don't want to disappoint Him. Once I get into the Bible, I feel renewed and eager to continue.

2. *Don't stray.* Some mornings I enjoy taking my little dog, Missy, along on my walk. Frequently I have to rein her in when she tries to take a shortcut or heads in the wrong direction. When I'm tempted to stray from the path that the Lord has set before me, I can feel Him tugging on my "leash." Like Missy, I've learned that it's less painful to heed the first tug than to be forcefully dragged away.

3. *Keep going.* Sometimes life's difficulties seem insurmountable. The best way to handle those trials is the same

way I attack the steep hills along my route: Take a deep breath and keep climbing. In spite of aching muscles, I know that because I've been exercising daily, my legs will carry me to the top. When I've been walking daily with the Lord, I know I'll find the strength to climb my mountains.

4. *Drink plenty of water.* To avoid dehydration during my walks, I carry water and pause frequently to drink. To avoid a dry spell in my spiritual life, I also need to drink frequently of God's "living water" through prayer and Bible study.

## Action 6: Deal with Depression

Despite your good intentions and best efforts, your husband may experience feelings of depression when he comes home for good. According to the National Foundation for Depressive Illness, a third of retirees experience occasional depression. One in six becomes depressed enough to require treatment.

How can you tell whether your mate is depressed? Look for these symptoms:[9]

- Poor appetite and trouble sleeping
- Persistent down mood
- Loss of interest in appearance, hygiene, and surroundings
- Trouble focusing and making decisions
- Irritability and conflict with others
- Desperation

If your husband is experiencing this last symptom, he needs immediate medical attention. For those who reach the desperation stage, nothing in life matters. Trying to cheer him up with promises that "this will pass" or urging him to "stop moping around" will not be effective and could even be harmful. He needs professional help. Don't wait for him to snap out of it; seek assistance from a counselor right away.

In less urgent cases of depression, you can help your husband—and yourself—by following the advice of Dr. Philip Alper as outlined in his article "Are You Singing the Retirement Blues?"[10]

*First, get a grip on yourself.* If you aren't careful, you may end up as depressed as your spouse.

*Let your mate know how you feel.* Depressed people are often unaware of the impact they have on others. But deliver your comments—which he may interpret as criticism—in small doses rather than overwhelming him.

*Never underestimate the power of love.* Showing you care may be the most important thing you can do. When your husband sees how much you love him, he'll start to see his value—and become motivated to work through his problems.

*Create your own support system.* A depressed husband can't give you the support and love you need. "If you feel deprived, it's probably because you are," writes Dr. Alper. Share your feelings with a trusted friend or counselor.

Find out whether a church in your area offers a support group for people suffering from depression. A caregivers' group may also be available.

If depression isn't a problem for your spouse right now, keep in mind that it could strike in the future. Here are some of Dr. Alper's tips for *avoiding* depression.[11]

*Find role models.* Among the retirees you know, whom would you like to emulate?

*Keep your expectations realistic.* Retirement is a time of give and take. Look for a balance between old and new; for example, moving to a retirement community might mean leaving old friends, but will also mean making new ones.

*Stay plugged into society.* Volunteering and joining clubs can help.

*Go easy on yourself.* A man who hasn't been on a golf

course in years, for instance, may have lost some of his skills. If all else fails, try something new.

*Use the computer to keep in touch with friends and grand-kids.* Unlike the telephone, e-mail neither intrudes on people's privacy nor requires an immediate answer. You don't have to be a computer whiz, either. As Dr. Alper notes, "Typing with two fingers doesn't break any laws."

Encourage your husband to seek fellowship with Christian friends. A weekly Bible study can be a great way to maintain friendships. Even an occasional morning out for coffee with a pal can be a big boost to a man's morale.

Daily exercise is another way to keep the blues away. Personally, I prefer the kind of "no-impact" workout I read about recently—jumping to conclusions, climbing the walls, pushing my luck, bending over backwards, and running around in circles. But to do some real good, you'll want to include some actual physical activity.

Remind your spouse to check with his doctor before beginning an exercise program. And be sure the two of you are eating nutritiously.

## On the Road Again

Did you hear about the man who retired and moved next to a public school? He was shocked to find that every afternoon a group of boys would bang on everyone's garbage cans during the walk home. The noise was bone-rattling.

But the retiree had an idea. One day he told the boys how much he loved to hear that noise—so much, in fact, that he'd pay them each a dollar a day to keep it up. The boys readily agreed.

A few days later, though, he met the rowdy bunch again. "I'm so sorry," he said, shaking his head. "My Social Security can't keep up with inflation. I'm afraid I can only pay you a quarter to make that lovely noise from now on."

"What?" cried the boys' leader. "You think we'll do this for a lousy quarter? Forget it!"

And from that day forward, the wise retiree had the peace and quiet he so richly deserved.

That man knew how to make the best of his new surroundings. We can help our spouses do the same.

There are bumps and potholes on all roads, even those that lead to wonderful destinations. Your husband will surely encounter some rough patches as he heads into retirement. Lessen his unease by reminding him that he's not alone on his journey; you are also struggling to adjust to a new lifestyle.

Together you can address each other's concerns. With your support and understanding, you and your mate can move toward your destination—a happy retirement.

# 12

# Thank You, Lord

֎֎

*It's not the outlook, but the uplook that counts.*
—AUTHOR UNKNOWN

Here we are, at the moment of truth.

In the first chapter I promised you that by the time you reached the end of this book, you'd be able to cherish your situation—or at least be grateful for it. Since then, you've seen how to accept the fact that your husband is home. You've probably aired some gripes and learned some coping skills. You've recognized your husband's needs and maybe even developed compassion for him.

Now I have to ask: Are you ready to cherish your situation?

That is, are you ready to consider the things for which you're grateful?

I hope that's a resounding "Yes!" I hear.

You can find plenty to be grateful for as you and your husband explore this new stage in your relationship. Sure, things have changed. But David and Claudia Arp offer this hopeful thought: "Changes, when handled wisely, can enhance a second-half marriage." They also note, "You can build a more intimate, personal relationship, if you are willing to change, focus on your partner and nurture your marriage. Good marriages are held together from within—from the inner core of the relationship." Their advice is to "refocus and become best friends."[1]

## Think, Thank, Tell

What is it about your "best friend" that endears him to you? Can you name a few things he did this week for which you're grateful? Or have you been too focused on the few things he *didn't* do right?

A lot of us may be doing just that. As comedian Red Skelton put it, "All men make mistakes, but married men find out about them sooner."

As for me, I'm learning to appreciate my husband and his way of doing things—even though it differs from mine. Take the speaker's conference I attended recently. To start with, I'd turned down Ken's offer to help me map the route to my destination; I claimed to know a "secret shortcut." After discovering my shortcut was no secret, I got to the hotel late. I threw my bags on the bed without unpacking, and without checking out the room's amenities—thereby breaking two of Ken's travel rules.

Since my worst fear is having to eat alone, I rushed to the lobby to find a dinner partner. I managed to find half a dozen, and spent mealtime gabbing with them instead of eating my cheese enchiladas. Hungry but out of time, I reluctantly refused the waiter's offer to box them up. "I have no way to reheat them," I explained.

Several hours later I spied the microwave in a far corner of my room—too late to do me any good, of course. It was also too late to get the wrinkles out of my now-unpacked suit. For the rest of the evening, I suffered a gnawing feeling—especially in my stomach—that I should have followed Ken's Perfect Personality rules instead of my Popular Personality ones.

Are you concentrating too much on your spouse's "downside"? That's what author Yvonne Turnbull was doing until she discovered three little words: *think, thank,* and *tell.*[2]

To help us *think* properly, she advises reading Philippians 4:8: "Finally, brothers, whatever is true, whatever is noble, whatever is right, whatever is pure, whatever is lovely, whatever is admirable—if anything is excellent or praiseworthy—think about such things."

This beautiful passage gets us started in the right direction. Yvonne suggests that, to counter critical thoughts about your spouse, you list 10 great things about him. She writes that when she asked the Lord to open her eyes to things that were right about her husband, "I noticed the many things about him that I had often overlooked or had taken for granted."

To help you *thank,* Yvonne recommends reading Ephesians 5:20, which reminds us to be "always giving thanks to God the Father for everything, in the name of our Lord Jesus Christ." She suggests that, for an entire week—once in the morning and once in the evening—you read the list of 10 great things about your husband. Thank God for each quality as you read it.

To *tell,* make a point of consistently offering verbal praise to your spouse. If he's used to being criticized, your new behavior may make him wonder if you're setting him up for something. In time, however, he'll get over his fear and realize that God is changing you.

Yvonne expresses gratitude to her husband, Bob, on paper, too. "I write him gratitude notes that start out with, 'Thank You, Lord, for Bob because . . .' Then I add something I observed or heard that day so that Bob will know."

I like her idea of counting your blessings instead of piling up grievances. A good place to record those blessings is a gratitude journal. You can make one with a simple spiral notebook, but most bookstores also stock journals that are geared specifically for recording grateful thoughts.

I gave my mother a gratitude journal on her 89th birthday. A few days later she called to tell me that she couldn't find five new things to list every day. "At my age," she joked, "about the only thing I'm grateful for is that my name wasn't listed in this morning's obituary column. Why, I don't even buy green bananas."

With a little encouragement, though, my mom developed a grateful eye. Recently her five items included these: a phone call from her granddaughter; completing a crossword puzzle with no help; not falling asleep before the ending of a *Perry Mason* episode; finding a misplaced recipe; and temperatures in two digits instead of three (she lives in the desert).

Once you get in the habit of looking for things to be thankful for, you'll view life—including your at-home spouse—in a wonderful, new way.

## Ode to an At-home Spouse

Even if you don't have a gratitude journal yet, why not grab pen and paper right now and write down five things about your husband for which you're grateful? After keeping a gratitude journal for several years, I developed such a thankful attitude about Ken that I penned this poem about him:

*The Mechanical Man*
I'm married to a marvelous, mechanical man,
Whose every move must first have a plan.
If I'm not penciled in his appointment book,
There is no use giving him that certain look.
His agenda is decided before he ever arises,
And he marches through life with few surprises.
While I find joy in unexpected pleasures,
Efficient schedules are his real treasures.
But I can't complain about my methodical man,
Because I'm the only woman who fits in his plan.

As my little composition plainly shows, you don't have to be a true poet to pen a verse. Just gather some thoughts about your husband, put pen to paper, and see what happens. While my poem is lighthearted, wives with romantic souls might come up with more amorous odes to their spouses. Writing about your husband—whether in a poem or a gratitude list— is a great way to rediscover your feelings for him.

## Love While You Can

A group of children, ages four to eight, were asked, "What does love mean?" These are some of their insightful answers:

"Love is when Mommy sees Daddy smelly and sweaty and still says he is handsomer than Robert Redford."

"Love is when a girl puts on perfume and a boy puts on shaving cologne and they go out and smell each other."

"Love is what makes you smile when you're tired."

"Love is when Mommy gives Daddy the best part of the chicken."

"Love is like a little old woman and a little old man who are still friends even after they know each other so well."

"When you love somebody, your eyelashes go up and down and little stars come out of you."

"You really shouldn't say 'I love you' unless you mean it. But if you mean it, you should say it a lot. People forget."

Don't *you* forget to say "I love you" to your husband, and say it a lot. Sadly, many men and women regret seldom having expressed their affection for a loved one while they had the chance.

In my nursing home ministry, I'm reminded of life's uncertainty. Our days on earth are numbered. Widows frequently tell me, "You know, I would give anything to have my husband around the house all day." So cherish your spouse. Always be grateful for the time God allows you to spend with him.

That great philosopher Winnie the Pooh said, "If you live to be a hundred, I want to live to be a hundred minus one day, so I never have to live without you." That's what it means to cherish someone.

It's been almost 11 years since Ken burst into our kitchen with that fax machine. Things have changed quite a bit. I have a new meatloaf pan—and a new, grateful attitude about my situation. Besides understanding what it means to cherish someone, Ken and I are both wiser about a few other "C" words as well—communication, compassion, and consideration.

But knowledge doesn't make us perfect. There are days

when I have to remind myself to "practice what I preach."
Those are the times when I cherish—my sense of humor!

Keep *your* sense of humor too.

Remember to practice your ABCs.

And always keep in mind a phrase my friend's mother
uses to close her letters:

*Take care of each other.*

To find out more about the author's workshops, or to contact
her, please visit her Web site at www.maryanncook.com.

# Appendix

# Ten Top Tips for Living with an At-home Husband

1. Form an open and honest partnership.

2. Help your spouse feel welcome and comfortable in your home.

3. Communicate clearly, keeping in mind your mate's personality.

4. Consider your mate's needs and desires, not just your own.

5. Look for the humor in every situation.

6. Speak kindly and respectfully to each other.

7. Provide escape hatches for the rough times.

8. Stay active with both separate and joint pursuits.

9. Make time for yourself and don't feel guilty.

10. Count your blessings and record them in a gratitude journal.

# Helpful Hints

I often ask at-home couples, "What works for you?" Here are some nuggets of wisdom gleaned from my interviews.

"Every day is a new start. Don't hold on to old grudges."

"I don't do breakfast or lunch. I never did them before; why should I start now?"

"I threw a New Beginnings party for my husband when he retired. Now we're having so much fun together that we haven't had time to think about the retired part yet."

"I think of him before I think of myself. He does the same thing. It can't be one-sided."

"When I need a breather from too much togetherness, I call my husband's best friend. He comes over and drags my husband off for lunch or a round of golf."

"We're considering selling our home and buying a duplex. We'll each have our own space, and we will get together at mealtimes."

"No matter how busy I am, if my husband needs me, I make sure I'm there for him."

"When I hear someone wish a bride and groom, 'Good luck,' I remind them that luck has nothing to do with it. A good marriage is hard work. But it's well worth the effort."

"Get a pet for your husband. It will give him a sense of purpose—and keep him out of your hair."

"We start every morning in prayer—before we even get out of bed. We praise God for His goodness and for whatever time we have left together."

# Success Stories

## Willy and William

William is a dairy farmer, so the work he does is often out on the "south forty." He and his wife, Willy, don't suffer from too much togetherness in quite the same way that most work-at-home spouses do.

The two labor as a team. William works the land and Willy works on the ledger sheets. William says he's grateful that his wife handles the bookkeeping. "That way I can do what I like best—farming. I don't have to worry about the business end of it," he explains.

Willy believes that having her husband close by on a daily basis enhances the communication between them. They always get together for a cup of coffee at 11 A.M. When something comes up, either good or bad, they can share the information immediately. "We don't have to wait until he gets home at the end of the day to take care of any problems that might arise," Willy says. "This way we don't let things fester; we take care of it right away."

Because their responsibilities are well-defined and mostly separate, there's seldom a need for compromise. While they do talk over most matters, they respect each other's decisions. "I trust her completely," William says.

Willy cites the addition of a screened-in back patio as an example of one of the few compromises her husband has had to make. She wanted him to feel comfortable in their home, but his muddy boots were making it difficult for her to keep the floors clean. So William closed in the patio off the dining room, where he can sit and relax in his dirty clothes and boots. "I can take off my boots and clean them before coming into the house," he explains.

Willy is grateful for his thoughtfulness. "I didn't want to be nitpicky about it. You have to decide what is really important—a clean house or your family."

Willy and William put serving the Lord at the top of their priorities. "We see pretty much eye to eye on everything," William says. On those rare occasions when they don't, and they sense irritability setting in, they think about it before they discuss the problem. They're honest with each other and usually say, "It bothered me when you . . ." But William adds, "We don't do this right away. I might go outside and work *really* hard for a while!"

As for separate or shared activities, this hardworking couple tries to make time for them. Willy enjoys playing the church organ, cross-stitching, reading, and taking care of the grandchildren. She also helps edit the alumni magazine for their local Christian high school.

"I don't need a hobby," her husband insists. "I have fun doing what I do on the farm." He loves finding ways to fix things. He also keeps busy with his work on the boards of several dairy organizations, and has served on the school board and church council.

The couple enjoys having family over in the evenings for board games and conversation. "A lot of laughs have been shared over this old dining room table," William says.

Willy's gratitude list includes the fact that her husband trusts and respects her. She also admires the patience he has with their children, and the fact that she can be sure of his love. "I see it in the way he supports me in everything," she says.

At the top of William's list is his wife's commitment to the Lord and their family. "I appreciate that she has always stood behind me in the raising of our kids," he says. He also admires her loving and caring attitude.

⊘⊘

**Al and Marionne**
You might call Marionne and Al the poster couple for retired folks. Married 55 years, they still act like lovebirds. "We both like to hug a lot," Al says. They often can be found strolling hand in hand along the beach, waiting for their "usual" table at a favorite seaside cafe. Marionne says she still finds her 76-year-old husband as attractive as the day she first spotted him.

Al took an early retirement in 1985; since then he and Marionne have enjoyed many of the leisure activities afforded by their community. Al spends a lot of his free time on the golf course, but also is involved in community theater.

Marionne says she never feared her husband's retirement the way some women do. "I was only concerned about how it might affect him," she confides.

Not surprisingly, these two can easily list things about each other for which they're grateful. Al says he appreciates Marionne's compatibility, her magnetic femininity, and her outstanding motherhood characteristics. The fact that she's a great cook is also high on his list of compliments.

Like Al, Marionne finds it hard to choose only three things about her husband for which she's grateful. These are the ones she finally settled on: "He has always been faithful and true. He always puts me first in his life, and has always been there when I needed him. He is a very gentle man."

Marionne says she considers herself lucky that her husband believes in letting her have her own space. She's free to pursue her own interests with friends, which include bridge, golfing, and Bible study.

When it comes to shared interests, their five grandchildren are at the top of their agenda. They make a point of inviting each child to their home for frequent visits, in addition to taking several trips a year to visit them. Their church is the center of many activities they participate in together.

Though they may spend time away from each other during the day, they always get together in the late afternoon for a long walk. In the evenings they enjoy having friends over, too.

The secret of this couple's success? Start with a large portion of love and sensitivity to each other's needs. Add an active lifestyle, freedom to pursue individual interests, and quality time together.

ⓔⓔ

### Ann and Gary

A retired Air Force officer, Gary finds satisfaction in his volunteer work as administrator for a Christian charitable medical clinic which he helped establish. His wife, Ann, is a former schoolteacher.

Shared common interests are part of the reason that Ann and Gary can be included on the list of couples enjoying retirement. They also believe it's important to have separate interests. Ann savors time to herself when she can read or go for a walk. She also enjoys cooking and volunteer work. When not at the clinic, Gary spends his free time doing yard work or woodworking projects. He lists his woodworking shed at the rear of the property as his escape hatch.

Escape hatches for Ann include a nearby hospital where she volunteers in the maternity ward, and the charitable medical clinic where she lends a hand with clerical work.

But for this couple, escape hatches are seldom needed. Gary and Ann remain compatible most of the time. Their explanation: strong Christian values, and the fact that they genuinely like each other. "We are best friends," Ann says.

It's not hard for these two, married 31 years, to name things about each other for which they're grateful. Gary's list: "The secure feeling that Ann really loves me. That she is a strong Christian. That she laughs at my silly jokes and puns."

That sense of humor is first on Ann's list of things about Gary for which she's grateful. Next comes the fact that he's a strong Christian, followed by, "He's true to me."

Like any married couple, Gary and Ann find that sometimes they get on each other's nerves. But they've found a way to work through it.

"If one of us is irritable, the other one seems to sense it and we give each other some space," Ann explains.

Though they share many interests when it comes to activities, Ann and Gary admit to being very different when it comes to personality traits. As an extrovert, Ann enjoys "working the room" in social settings; Gary is more comfortable chatting with one or two people.

The biggest difference between the two involves the save-versus-toss issue. Gary is a pack rat, while Ann admits to throwing out anything for which she can't see a need. This could be a real source of contention between the two, if they weren't willing to compromise. Ann pretty much decides how the house is organized, while Gary rules his workshop. He also has a bedroom closet that is off-limits to Ann's search-and-destroy campaign. "I just look the other way," Ann explains.

Ann sees their differences as an advantage: "My strengths are his weaknesses, and his strengths are my weaknesses."

✪✪

## Marilyn and Ken

This couple got a taste of living together 24/7 during the summers when Ken was on vacation from his job as an elementary school teacher.

"We realized right away that for both of our sakes, a part-time job after retirement would be a good idea," Marilyn says. So before he retired from his teaching job eight years ago, Ken started a locksmith business which he operated on weekends. After his retirement he added one weekday to his work schedule. The rest of the week is free for him and Marilyn to indulge in their favorite pastime, long drives in the country.

When not exploring together, Marilyn and Ken enjoy church activities, watching old movies on TV on "Popcorn Night," and working in the yard—especially those long breaks when they settle in the shade of the patio for lemonade, Marilyn confesses.

For separate activities, Ken chooses his part-time job. Marilyn volunteers at a nursing home and helps to raise funds for a church camp.

Ken and Marilyn find that giving each other space is the answer when they get on each other's nerves. Ken's favorite escape hatch is Home Depot; Marilyn takes off for the mall or lunch with friends.

While some couples find it difficult to compromise when making important decisions, Marilyn and Ken say they don't mind the give-and-take. They find compromise especially important when making vacation plans. "We can usually talk anything out and come to a joint decision," Ken explains.

Faith, respect, and love for each other are at the top of this couple's list of what it takes to have a successful relationship. Among qualities to be grateful for, Marilyn names Ken's genuineness. "What you see is what you get," she says. As for Ken, he appreciates Marilyn's loving ways and her organizational skills. What they both like most about each other is being best friends.

Ken and Marilyn offer the following advice to at-home couples:

- Plan ahead!
- Strike a balance between activities you share and those you pursue separately.
- Don't try to dominate the other person when it comes to what he or she does or doesn't want to do.
- Communicate well. It's extremely important to be able to discuss everything with each other.

# Recommended Reading

**FOR UNDERSTANDING:**
*Every Day Is Saturday*
L. James and Jackie Harvey
Concordia Publishing House, 2000

*Getting Along with Almost Anybody*
Florence Littauer and Marita Littauer
Fleming H. Revell, 1998

*Growing Older Together*
Barbara Silverstone and Helen Kandel Hyman
Thorndike Press, 1992 (large print edition)

*Help Me, I'm Married!*
Joyce Meyer
Harrison House, 2001

*How to Get Your Husband to Talk to You*
Nancy Cobb and Connie Grigsby
Multnomah Publishers, 2001

*How to Live with Them Since You Can't Live Without Them*
Becky Tirabassi and Roger Tirabassi
Thomas Nelson, 1998

*Keys to Living with a Retired Husband*
Gloria Bledsoe Goodman

Barron's Educational Series
(out of print—look for used copies at bookstores or on the Internet)

*Men Are from Mars, Women Are from Venus*
John Gray, Ph.D.
Harper Collins, 1992

*Men Are Like Waffles, Women Are Like Spaghetti*
Bill and Pam Farrel
Harvest House, 2001

*Personality Plus for Couples*
Florence Littauer
Fleming H. Revell, 2001
(includes personality test)

*The Language of Love*
Gary Smalley and John Trent, Ph.D.
Focus on the Family/Tyndale, 1991

*The Power of a Praying Wife*
Stormie Omartian
Harvest House, 1997

*You Just Don't Understand*
Deborah Tannen, Ph.D.
Ballantine Books, 1990

**FOR INSPIRATION:**
*Add Life to Your Years*
Ted W. Engstrom and Joy B. Gage
Tyndale House, 2002

*A Woman's Journey to the Heart of God*
Cynthia Heald
Thomas Nelson, 1997

*Gift from the Sea*
Anne Morrow Lindbergh
Pantheon Books, 1991

*God's Little Instruction Book*
Honor Books, 1996

*Moments Together for Couples*
Dennis and Barbara Rainey
Regal Books, 1995

*Night Light*
Dr. James and Shirley Dobson
Multnomah Publishers, 2000

*OverJoyed!*
Patsy Clairmont, Barbara Johnson, Marilyn Meberg, Luci
Swindoll, Sheila Walsh, Thelma Wells
Zondervan, 1999
(also good for laughs)


**FOR LAUGHS:**
*A Marriage Made in Heaven . . . or Too Tired for an Affair*
Erma Bombeck
Harper Mass Market Paperbacks, 1994

*Don't Squat with Yer Spurs On!*
Texas Bix Bender
Gibbs Smith, 1992

*Help! I'm Laughing and I Can't Get Up*
Liz Curtis Higgs
Thomas Nelson, 1998

*Living Somewhere Between Estrogen and Death*
Barbara Johnson
Word Publishing, 1997

*Sometimes I Wake Up Grumpy. . . and Sometimes I Let Him Sleep*
Karen Scalf Linamen
Fleming H. Revell, 2001

*Normal Is Just a Setting on Your Dryer*
Patsy Clairmont
Focus on the Family, 1993

*The Wit and Wisdom of Women*
Melissa Stein
Running Press, 1993
(Also good for inspiration)

# Where to Get Help

**AARP**
601 E. Street N.W.
Washington, D.C. 20049
(800) 424-3410 (membership)
(888) AARP-NOW (tax-aid site locator and "55 Alive" mature driving program)
Web site: www.aarp.org
　　AARP is a nonprofit membership organization for people 50 and over. Publications are available on housing, health, exercise, retirement planning, money management, leisure, and travel.

**Christian Association of PrimeTimers (CAP)**
P.O. Box 777
St. Charles, IL 60174-0777
(800) 443-0227
Web site: www.christianprimetimers.org
　　This organization is a Christian alternative to AARP.

**Christian Seniors Fellowship**
P.O. Box 46464
Cincinnati, OH 45246
(800) 35-ALIVE (352-5483)
Web site: www.missionsalive.org/csf
　　With *Alive!* magazine, conferences, and materials, this organization strives to evangelize, revitalize, and equip seniors for ministry and service for Christ.

## CLASS

The personality test mentioned in chapter 6 is included in the book *Personality Plus for Couples* (see Recommended Reading); or you may order a test from CLASS at:
(800) 433-6633
Web site: www.thepersonalities.com

## Focus on the Family

8605 Explorer Drive
Colorado Springs, CO 80920
(719) 531-3400
(800) A-FAMILY (for orders)
Web site: www.family.org

Focus on the Family publishes *LifeWise* magazine as part of its "Focus over Fifty" ministry. See the Web site for other resources as well.

Focus on the Family also provides professional counseling (a free, one-time service by phone) and referrals to Christian counselors nationwide. The phone line is open weekdays, 9 A.M. to 4:40 P.M. mountain time; ask for the counseling department at extension 2700.

## Home Office Association of America (HOAA)

P.O. Box 51
Sagaponack, NY 11962-0051
(800) 809-4622
Web site: www.hoaa.com

This organization offers services to home-based and small business professionals, with member benefits including a newsletter and group savings on health insurance.

## National Council on the Aging (NCOA)
(800) 424-9046

Web site: www.ncoa.org

NCOA is a national information and consultation center. Here one can find information on adult care centers, senior housing, financial issues, and services for seniors. Books, brochures, and pamphlets are offered.

## National Foundation for Depressive Illness (NAFDI)
P.O. Box 2257

New York, NY 10116

(800) 239-1265

Web site: www.depression.org

NAFDI provides information on recent advances in treatment. It also offers referrals to doctors who treat depression.

## Oasis
(314) 862-2933

Web site: www.oasisnet.org

This national nonprofit organization is designed to enhance the quality of life for mature adults. It offers programs in the arts, humanities, wellness, technology, and volunteer services. Visit their Web site to find a local chapter.

## SOHO America, Inc.
P.O. Box 941

Hurst, TX 76053-0941

(800) 495-SOHO

Web site: www.soho.org

SOHO stands for "Small Office/Home Office." This organization's Web site offers a newsletter, articles, and other information. Note that SOHO prefers to be contacted online rather than through "snail mail."

**United Seniors Association**
3900 Jermantown Road #450
Fairfax, VA 22030
(800) 887-2872
Web site: www.unitedseniors.org
   This nonprofit organization is "the leading group for citizen activists who want to cut taxes, safeguard the Social Security Trust Fund, and improve Social Security and Medicare for all generations."

**United Seniors Health Council**
409 Third Street, S.W.
Washington, D.C. 20024
(202) 479-6678
Web site: www.unitedseniorshealth.org
   This organization helps older consumers, caregivers, and professionals through a wide range of programs and services, including publications on financial planning, home care, long-term-care insurance, and other topics.


(Note: The preceding resources and organizations offer helpful information, but not all the views expressed by all of them are necessarily endorsed by Focus on the Family.)

# Notes

## Chapter 2: Here to Stay

1. Margaret Mead, quoted by Barbara Silverstone and Helen Kandal Hyman, *Growing Older Together* (Thorndike, Minn.: Thorndike Press, 1992), p. 25.
2. Silverstone and Hyman, p. 21.
3. Anne Morrow Lindbergh, *Gift from the Sea* (New York: Pantheon Books, 1991), pp. 108-109.

## Chapter 3: Howdy, Pardner

1. Susan Littwin, "Your Marriage May Never Be the Same Again," *New Choices* (March 1998): 63.
2. Norm Wakefield and Jody Brolsma, *Men Are from Israel, Women Are from Moab* (Downers Grove, Ill.: InterVarsity Press, 2000), p. 57.
3. Ibid., p. 54.
4. Roger Fisher and William Ury, *Getting to Yes: Negotiating Agreement Without Giving In* (New York: Penguin Group, 1983), p. 42.
5. Joyce Meyer, *Help Me, I'm Married!* (Tulsa, Okla.: Harrison House, Inc., 2000), p. 239.
6. *Webster's Ninth New Collegiate Dictionary* (Springfield, Mass.: Merriam-Webster, 1984), p. 859.
7. Littwin, p. 62.
8. Ruth Bell Graham, "Making a Marriage Work," *Decision* (February 2000): 20.
9. Gloria Bledsoe Goodman, *Keys to Living with a Retired Husband* (Hauppauge, N.Y.: Barron's Educational Series, 1991), p. 49.

## Chapter 4: He Drives Me Crazy

1. Texas Bix Bender, *Don't Squat with Yer Spurs On!* (Salt Lake City: Gibbs Smith, 1992), p. 82. Used with permission.
2. Claudia Arp and Dave Arp, "Is Your Spouse Driving You Nuts?" *Today's Christian Woman* (March/April 1995): 56.

## Chapter 5: I Want to Be Alone

1. Stormie Omartian, *The Power of a Praying Wife* (Eugene, Ore.: Harvest House, 1997), p. 32.
2. Ibid., pp. 32-33.

## Chapter 6: Failures to Communicate

1. Silverstone and Hyman, p. 77.
2. Shelby Hearon, "Your Mate Has Changed—Cherish It," *New Choices* (December 1997/January 1998): 66.
3. Susan Lenzkes, "Lend Me an Ear," *Women's Devotional Bible,* New International Version (Grand Rapids, Mich.: Zondervan, 1995), p. 1395.
4. Lysa TerKeurst, *Capture Her Heart* (Chicago: Moody Press, 2002), pp. 65-66.
5. John Gray, *Men Are from Mars, Women Are from Venus* (New York: Harper Collins, 1992), p. 88.
6. Ibid., p. 89.
7. Bill and Pam Farrel, *Men Are Like Waffles, Women Are Like Spaghetti* (Eugene, Ore.: Harvest House, 2001), p. 11.
8. Ibid.
9. Ibid., pp. 13-14.
10. TerKeurst, pp. 66-67.
11. Farrel, p. 37.
12. Joyce Meyer, *Help Me, I'm Married!* (Tulsa, Okla.: Harrison House, Inc., 2000), p. 158.

13. Ibid.
14. Ibid.
15. Gary Smalley and John Trent, Ph.D., *The Language of Love* (Wheaton, Ill.: Focus on the Family/Tyndale House, 1991), p. 35.
16. Deborah Tannen, *You Just Don't Understand* (New York: Ballantine Books, 1990), p. 77.
17. Ibid., p. 15
18. Florence Littauer and Marita Littauer, *Personality Puzzle* (Grand Rapids, Mich.: Fleming H. Revell, 1992). Information from *Personality Plus for Couples* by Florence Littauer © 2001 by Florence Littauer. Used by permission of Florence Littauer and Fleming H. Revell Company. Not to be reproduced. Copies of *Personality Plus for Couples* and Personality Profiles may be ordered from CLASS, P.O. Box 66810, Albuquerque, NM 87193-6810. Credit card orders may be placed by contacting www.thepersonalities.com or, in the U.S., by calling 1-800-433-6633.

## Chapter 7: Laughing Matters

1. Patsy Clairmont, quoted in *Applause* (March 4, 2000), a weekly update published by CLASServices, Inc.
2. Sebastian Roché, quoted in *God's Little Instruction Book for Women* (Tulsa, Okla.: Honor Books, Inc., 1996), p. 46.

## Chapter 9: No More Couch Potatoes

1. Goodman, p. 29.
2. Marc Freedman, "The New Unretirement," *Modern Maturity* (January/February 2001): 54.
3. Ibid.

## Chapter 11: Relishing Retirement

1. Philip R. Alper, "Are You Singing the Retirement Blues?" *New Choices* (July/August 1998): 63.
2. Goodman, p. 27.
3. Silverstone and Hyman, pp. 223-24.
4. Ibid., p. 225.
5. L. James and Jackie Harvey, *Every Day Is Saturday* (St. Louis, Mo.: Concordia Publishing House, 2000), p. 132.
6. Ibid., p. 21.
7. Ibid.
8. Donna Schaper, "Get Ready," *These Days* (April–June 2002): April 11 devotion.
9. Alper, pp. 64-65.
10. Ibid., p. 63.
11. Ibid., p. 64.

## Chapter 12: Thank You, Lord

1. David Arp and Claudia Arp, "Move Your Marriage off the Back Burner," *Lifewise* (February/March 2001): 19.
2. Yvonne Turnbull, "Three Ways to Nurture a Marriage," *Decision* (February 2001): back page.

# FOCUS ON THE FAMILY

## $\mathcal{W}$elcome to the $\mathcal{F}$amily!

Whether you received this book as a gift, borrowed it from a friend, or purchased it yourself, we're glad you read it! It's just one of the many helpful, insightful, and encouraging resources produced by Focus on the Family.

In fact, that's what Focus on the Family is all about—providing inspiration, information, and biblically based advice to people in all stages of life.

It began in 1977 with the vision of one man, Dr. James Dobson, a licensed psychologist and author of 16 best-selling books on marriage, parenting, and family. Alarmed by the societal, political, and economic pressures that were threatening the existence of the American family, Dr. Dobson founded Focus on the Family with one employee—an assistant—and a once-a-week radio broadcast, aired on only 36 stations.

Now an international organization, Focus on the Family is dedicated to preserving Judeo-Christian values and strengthening the family through more than 70 different ministries, including eight separate daily radio broadcasts; television public service announcements; 10 publications; and a steady series of books and award-winning films and videos for people of all ages and interests.

Recognizing the needs of, as well as the sacrifices and important contributions made by, such diverse groups as educators, physicians, attorneys, crisis pregnancy center staff, and single parents, Focus on the Family offers specific outreaches to uphold and minister to these individuals, too. And it's all done for one purpose, and one purpose only: to encourage and strengthen individuals and families through the life-changing message of Jesus Christ.

•  •  •

For more information about the ministry, or if we can be of help to your family, simply write to Focus on the Family, Colorado Springs, CO 80995 or call 1-800-A-FAMILY (1-800-232-6459). Friends in Canada may write Focus on the Family, P.O. Box 9800, Stn. Terminal, Vancouver, B.C. V6B 4G3 or call 1-800-661-9800. Visit our Web site—www.family.org—to learn more about Focus on the Family or to find out if there is an associate office in your country.

We'd love to hear from you!

# More Gifts From the Heart
## *From Focus on the Family!*®

### Capture His Heart

Men are exciting. God made them that way! But many women find them frustrating and hard to figure out. And too often, there's unnecessary heartache and distance that creeps into marriages over time. Here's help: put your expectations and disappointments aside, and set out on a new adventure...a journey to understand, accept and love the heart of your husband!

### Capture Her Heart

Men find women fascinating. But while they may be captivated by the "feminine mystique," they also are often baffled by how to effectively communicate with and cherish their wives. Having a great marriage takes time, creativity and a willingness to understand the needs of the other person. This practical, "quick read" will give every husband great insights into the heart of his wife!

### The Love List

Relationship experts Drs. Les and Leslie Parrott draw on professional insights into successful marriages plus a candid look at their own marriage to give you eight simple-but-powerful principles that will lift your marriage out of the doldrums. The Love List isn't so much a "to do" list but a map of your journey together . . . daily, weekly, monthly and yearly. Don't put off the fun and fulfillment . . . start today!

### Heart to Heart Stories for Grandparents

This moving collection of stories, compiled by beloved master storyteller Joe Wheeler, focuses on the bond between grandparents and grandchildren. Its timeless themes of love and the strength of family ties will encourage and inspire you—whether you read them alone or out loud with a loved one.

●   ●   ●